Three
European Directors

Three European Directors

FRANÇOIS TRUFFAUT—
                                    James M. Wall

FELLINI'S FILM JOURNEY —
                                    Roger Ortmayer

**LUIS BUNUEL
AND THE DEATH OF GOD—**
                                    Peter P. Schillaci

edited by
James M. Wall

WILLIAM B. EERDMANS PUBLISHING COMPANY
Grand Rapids, Michigan

Printed in the United States of America

Library of Congress Cataloging in Publication Data

Wall, James McKendree, 1928–
    Three European directors.

    Includes bibliographies.
    1. Truffaut, François.   2. Fellini, Federico.
3. Buñuel, Luis, 1900–   I. Ortmayer, Roger.
II. Schillaci, Peter P., 1927–   III. Title.
PN1998.A2W33   796.43'092'2   72-84010
ISBN 0-8028-1504-9

Preface

The prime function of art is to make the felt tensions of life stand still to be looked at.

Susanne Langer

Art is the ability given to man to separate a form from the swirling chaos of his sensations, and to contemplate that form in its uniqueness.

Sir Herbert Read

The poetic imagination is the divinely given instrument by which men are able to apprehend, express and communicate the mystery of the world and of human life.

Alan Richardson

The point of this book is that movies can be more than entertainment—they can be the deep personal expression of an artist. The three men chosen for this study—all of them Europeans—are not formula directors locked into a production-line commitment to make the Big Profit, but serious artists committed to offering a vision, a profound and distinctive view of reality that can catch the viewer up in a revelatory experience.

Because, however, the vast majority of motion pictures are geared to a commercial market uninterested in film as art, many viewers find it difficult to cope with films made by cinematic artists. In presenting these essays on Truffaut, Fellini, and Bunuel, we wish to help the reader

5

perceive in their films depths of experience he might otherwise miss. The films considered in this book include works released through early 1973. While these directors will undoubtedly continue to make films (though Bunuel at seventy-three has talked of retiring), the following studies should be of value in interpreting their future efforts as well.

Finally, we hope that in helping the viewer better understand these established artists, we will also enable him to respond appreciatively to those younger, less known directors—both in the United States and in Europe—who are no less concerned to "apprehend, express and communicate" in film "the mystery of the world and of human life."

—James M. Wall
The Christian Century

Contents

FRANÇOIS TRUFFAUT

FELLINI'S FILM JOURNEY

LUIS BUNUEL AND THE DEATH OF GOD

FRANÇOIS TRUFFAUT
Auteur of Ambiguity

James M. Wall

Introduction

When François Truffaut began making feature films in 1958, "movies," as they are known in popular parlance, were not widely considered material for serious study. Truffaut had to help create a climate in which his kind of personal films could obtain a hearing. Research on Truffaut is in itself a short course in film history, language, and style, for Truffaut is not only a filmmaker, but a film scholar of considerable renown. In this he is somewhat different from most of his older colleagues in the United States, who are filmmakers but lack any real awareness of the history of their own medium. With Truffaut we are dealing with a film sensibility. He has a wide interest in, and concern for, the totality of film culture. To examine Truffaut in the light of this totality is to recognize that already in his early forties and after only eleven feature films, he has achieved a permanent place among film artists. If we may allude to a film technique he himself has used so effectively in his films, this presentation is a freeze-frame shot of Truffaut as he heads into the second decade of his professional career as a feature filmmaker.

A reader new to film study should be reminded of a peculiar circumstance surrounding a study of this sort. Anyone making a study of Ernest Hemingway's novels can turn quickly and easily from reading about Hemingway to an examination of the man's own work. With film study—at least until cassettes are perfected—we are not so fortunate. Many readers will not have seen all of Truffaut's films, and the reader cannot just pick up a Truffaut film and check his own observations against those that appear here. This is the burden of the film medium, an expensive vehicle to make, distribute, and show, and it is one of the reasons why our culture has failed to take film study seriously.

The dedicated film buff will work against this handicap, taking a certain fiendish pleasure at discovering one of his favorites at an out-of-the-way theater, or brought back on the bottom of a double bill, or playing at a nearby college campus. It is difficult to find your favorites, and the vagaries of the American film distribution system indicate almost no awareness of film as an art form. To recall the kind of advertising that has lured thrill-seekers to the fragile, sensitive works of Truffaut brings shudders. Exhibitors (with some happy exceptions) want to sell tickets, and since they rightly assume that film buffs don't exist in large enough numbers to pay the "nut" (trade talk for overhead), they sell Truffaut and others on the basis of what sells to the general public—sex and violence.

Chasing Truffaut films takes one from coast to coast. *The 400 Blows* and Truffaut's second film, *Shoot the Piano Player,* have been on the late night television circuit, and I must confess that my first exposure to each left me somewhat unimpressed. They were dubbed, which meant that the subtle French language rhythm was lost, replaced by wooden voices obviously reading in a studio, seldom with any real feeling for the script. Truffaut's third film, *Jules and Jim,* came to me in more direct fashion, as part of a college film series. Prints of all three of these titles are available from Janus Films, which has exclusive 16 mm rental distribution rights. (Further rental information on Truffaut's films may be found in the filmography, pp. 57ff.)

The Bride Wore Black appeared in a dubbed version as part of a double bill in a suburb near my home. It played, amazingly enough, with Ingmar Bergman's *Hour of the*

Wolf, and the dubbing effectively ruined two works of art. *Stolen Kisses* I saw at an out-of-the-way theater in New York; it was also in New York that I managed to see *Bed and Board* and *Mississippi Mermaid.* I viewed *The Wild Child* in the best possible circumstances, a press screening by the New York Film Festival. Truffaut himself was present for a press conference, answering inane questions about iris shots and about "Whatever happened to the boy?" *Fahrenheit 451,* Truffaut's sole English-language effort and possibly for that reason one of his less successful pictures, I had to catch at a matinee in Peoria, Illinois, between speaking assignments. *Soft Skin* was screened through a distributor's kind assistance. *Two English Girls* was the easiest yet, and I caught it at a theater screening in Chicago.

All this is simply to suggest that if the author himself has this much trouble following film artists, he cannot expect his readers to be thoroughly familiar with the works under discussion. However, even given all the chasing, nothing can compare with repeated viewings of Truffaut's films. Later viewings of *Jules and Jim,* for example, reveal touches of cinematic sensitivity that are almost impossible to find the first time around. I hope this essay will provide something of a first viewing of Truffaut's films, so that subsequent viewings of his work, including screenings of his new works, will be enriched.

1

The Auteurs

François Truffaut first met Alfred Hitchcock when
that great master of the suspense film came to France to
complete location shooting on *To Catch a Thief* in the
winter of 1955. Truffaut was a twenty-three-year-old film
buff, would-be film critic, former deserter from the
French Army, and Hitchcock fan. He and Claude Chabrol
were working for the French critical journal *Cahiers du
Cinema,* a publication that would become the originator
and sustainer of a theory of film criticism based on an
understanding of the film director as the "author" *(auteur)* of his picture. Armed with a tape recorder and a
heavy dose of hero worship, Truffaut and Chabrol approached Hitchcock in a darkened screening room where
loops (repeated shots) of *Thief* were running. He asked
them to meet him later at a bar across the way. As
Truffaut recalls it, "We emerged into the blinding glare of
daylight, literally bursting with excitement." Hitchcock,
after all, was one of the authentic masters of modern
cinema. But in the heat of their discussion together, the
two young Frenchmen failed to notice a frozen pond in
the middle of the studio courtyard. They fell through the
ice, soaking their clothes, ruining their tape recorder, and
seriously jeopardizing the crucial meeting with Hitchcock. Looking back, Truffaut remembers the image they
created: "Staggering around the sloping basin, unable to
reach the edge without sliding right back to the center,

we were trapped in a situation straight out of a Hitchcock movie."[1]

When they finally escaped and made their way to the appointed bar, Hitchcock graciously suggested a later and more relaxed interview. From this beginning, Truffaut's relationship with Hitchcock has been influential on his work, though not on his personal vision. The Frenchman admires Hitchcock as the "world's foremost technician," a director determined to "keep banality off the screen." Seven years after his plunge into the studio pool, Truffaut persuaded Hitchcock to sit still for fifty hours of interviews in Hollywood, from which Truffaut developed a remarkably readable and helpful film book, *Hitchcock*, examining in detail every film Hitchcock has made. But Truffaut's questions and observations reveal as much about his own style as they do about Hitchcock's, suggesting that he shares with Hitchcock an intense desire to express himself in visual terms and to communicate with audiences. In this, Truffaut differs from some filmmakers of his generation, who feel that the "art" film doesn't have to make sense to an audience so long as it expresses a personal vision. Some may be inclined to charge that Truffaut wants to sell his pictures, and aspects of his films do appear to be commercially motivated. For example, the plots of *Mississippi Mermaid* and *The Bride Wore Black* are from routine novels—commercially exploitable, trivial, and even foolish on the surface. But it is not commerce Truffaut is after. Otherwise, he would have included overt nudity in his films during these years when national censor offices were relaxing their strictures. He also would not have made a film so completely uncommercial as *The Wild Child*.

No, Truffaut, like Hitchcock, wants to communicate. Some filmmakers use movies to tell stories, to stir emotions, or simply to exploit a subject (sex, drugs, war,

---

1. From the Introduction to Truffaut's *Hitchcock* (New York: Simon and Schuster, 1967), p. 9.

violence). But Truffaut uses film to communicate a personal vision. Incidentally, using the terms "film" and "movies" in this way is deliberate. In the film culture, a "movie" is an entertainment vehicle to which you go; a "film" is a cinematic experience.

Truffaut's love of the film medium began early, and it was a love closely related to his own troubled childhood. When France was liberated at the close of World War II, he was already a confirmed school dropout. *The 400 Blows* tells of his own childhood experience, not literally but in spirit. He admits to being a rejected child, living for the first eight years of his life with his grandmother, placed in her care by parents who were not "bad people," just "nervous and busy."[2] "My father," he recalls, "had only one thing on his mind, camping. My mother was embittered. No doubt she would have liked a more brilliant sort of life." They enrolled their son in a school at Rollin, and the young François promptly began playing hookey. "I started out by doing what the others did, and then I really acted up." The more he was punished, the more trouble he made. After moving from one school to another, constantly playing hookey to see movies, he and a friend decided one day that they had skipped school so many times they dared not return without a strong and valid excuse. It was 1943, and Truffaut's uncle had just been arrested by the Germans. This gave him the idea to tell school officials that his father had been arrested, gaining him sympathy and time. Unfortunately, however, his father showed up at school, blowing his cover and leading him to run away from home. He slept in subway shelters, stealing food and wine. Eventually his father found him, and with the boy's full dossier now known to school authorities, he was officially pegged as a troublemaker.

I have provided this report of Truffaut's early life not

2. *The 400 Blows*, filmscript by Truffaut, book edited by David Denby (New York: Grove, 1959), p. 216.

to probe for Freudian sources behind his creativity, but
to point out how completely autobiographical is his *The
400 Blows*. In that film—a sensitive examination of a thir-
teen-year-old boy's fall from an unhappy home life to reform
school—Truffaut obviously draws from his own experience. He used a young boy named Jean-Pierre Leaud,
who bears at least a slight resemblance to Truffaut, as a
truant who tells school officials he missed school because
his mother had died. In the film it is the boy's mother
who comes to check on her runaway child, ruining a brief
moment of sympathy he had received from an otherwise
overbearing teacher.

One of Truffaut's close companions throughout his
early years was Robert Lachenay (they were later united
professionally, Lachenay serving as assistant director for
Blows). It was in Lachenay's home that Truffaut lived
after yet another escape from his home. The two formed
the Film Addicts' Club, launched with a single print they
purchased of an old silent classic, *Metropolis*. The youthful adventure faltered, but with the arrogance and naiveté
of the young they blamed the failure on what they
considered their competition, another cine-club nearby.
Truffaut, movie lover and youthful delinquent, marched
over to the club to suggest a change in showing times. He
did not succeed in his immediate goal, but the visit was
profoundly significant to his personal and his future
professional life. The head of the other cine-club was
Andre Bazin, critic, scholar, and film lover, who had
formed the club during the war as part of a program to
care for young students thrown out of their scholastic
routines by the war. The thirty-year-old Bazin talked to
his youthful visitor, found in him a shared love of film,
and sent him back to his own Film Addicts' Club to keep
trying, in spite of the opposition. When Truffaut's father
finally caught up with his runaway son, he had him
arrested (as much an act of frustration as of anger) and
placed in a house of correction. Again, this incident is
paralleled in *The 400 Blows,* where the young Antoine

Doinel is put in a reform school after spending the night in a Paris lockup. One of the film's many memorable scenes shows Doinel's stoical face staring out from one of those wire cages that serve as temporary restrainers for prostitutes, thieves, and runaway boys caught on the streets of Paris.

Incarcerated in what Truffaut recalls as "half an insane asylum and half a house of correction," he faced a bleak future. But something had happened in his visit with Bazin, something that was of course related to their common love of films. Truffaut says quite simply, "I was saved by Andre Bazin." Already a critic of some public standing, Bazin was able to obtain Truffaut's release and secure him a job with Travail et Culture (Work and Culture), an organization begun by veterans of the resistance movement to sponsor cultural activities. It was a measure of Truffaut's parents' lack of interest—or possibly of their sense of inadequacy—that they turned over any legal responsibilities they had to their son. Truffaut's own autobiographical film of his childhood offers a remarkably sensitive and nonjudgmental view of his own parents. The fault of the elder Doinels in the film is not that they dislike their son, but that they are self-centered and personally inadequate to the task of raising a boy with such an introspective, rebellious nature. This view of his own parents is obviously slanted the way any case history would be described—more favorable to the boy than to his parents, but it is still not a hostile statement against his parents. More clues are available in later Truffaut films. For example, there is a particularly interesting and possibly revealing moment in *Bed and Board,* the third film in what is so far a trilogy of Doinel, in which the adult Antoine tells his wife that he is writing a novel about his own life. She remarks that he may be telling the world about his parents in a prejudiced manner. Truffaut may feel, then, that three films about Doinel-Truffaut are enough and represent too much the slanted view of youth. If indeed this is Truffaut's view, he is probably being overly sensitive, for given the facts of his youth, his parents are presented in a much more positive light than one might expect from an artist seeking to recover from childhood rejections.

In any event, Bazin clearly became the father figure Truffaut never had in his own parent. A brief look at Bazin at this point is in order. Afflicted with a disease that took his life at forty, Bazin possessed what his translator Hugh Gray termed "a passion for culture and truth, allied to a moral authority which gave him the command over others that he exercised over himself—not only throughout a long inner spiritual conflict but also throughout a heroic struggle with the disease that was to take him off at the height of his intellectual powers."[3] Bazin brought respectability to cinema, combining a love of the medium with a profound intellect. A writing colleague, Guy Leger, recalls the impact Bazin's approach to cinema had on him:

> What had been for me up to then only a pastime now began to appear, under the tutelage of Andre, a product of the age of the image, something that needed study if one was to savor its true flavor and understand its real significance; to make out its true language and to discover its objective laws.[4]

Bazin had hoped to be a teacher, but suffered from a stammer and so was denied a post. Writing about film gave his massive intellect the outing it needed. Critic P. A. Touchard said of him: "No one had a greater command of words than this man who stammered when he spoke— and who had likewise a fantastic appetite for the consumption of scientific, philosophical, and abstract terms. Yet he was in no sense a pedant, remaining ever in command of the appropriate use of all these terms."[5] To

3. From the Introduction to Bazin's *What Is Cinema?* (Berkeley: University of California, 1967).
4. *What Is Cinema?*, p. 2.
5. *What Is Cinema?*, p. 2.

an American public accustomed to gossip columns about stars and reviews about plots, an intellectual writing on cinema is a strange phenomenon. Certainly, Bazin's essay on "The Ontology of the Photographic Image" is the stuff of which academic disciplines are born and a far point from the "movies-are-entertainment" mentality.

Bazin died on November 11, 1958, one day after Truffaut began shooting on *The 400 Blows*. Thus he did not live long enough to see his young protégé emerge as one of the world's leading directors, but he must certainly have been aware of the potential talent in this waif from the streets who so desperately needed the stimulus and strength of a cinema-loving father figure. As viewers of the Doinel trilogy are aware, Truffaut-Doinel did not step into immediate maturity. At first there were the series of odd jobs, the constant movie going, and finally an incident Truffaut reveals in an episode in *Love at Twenty*, in which a young teenager spies on the girl he loves from a hotel across the street. "But," as Truffaut recalls, "I got tired of seeing her go to movies with other guys, so I enlisted in the Army."[6]

The French were fighting in Indo-China at the time, and after six months Truffaut received his orders to the front. On leave he decided he'd had enough of the army, and didn't go back. Penniless and without civilian clothes, he wandered the streets of Paris again, until he encountered some of his former cine-club friends, who quickly notified Bazin. As Truffaut remembers it:

> Bazin persuaded me to turn myself in and go on sick call. I was sent to Villemain hospital. I smoked cotton and aspirin cigarettes so my heartbeat would go way up, but they decided to send me to Germany anyway. Some pals of mine had lent me some books. I wanted to give the books back before I left, and as I was returning them, I once again

6. From an interview in *L'Express*, April 23, 1959, reprinted in the Grove Press edition of *The 400 Blows*, p. 219.

decided not to go back. But they came and got me and I
left for Germany in handcuffs.[7]

Like his parents, the army, too, finally gave up on him,
and he was discharged for "instability of character." This
experience is told in the opening scenes of *Stolen Kisses*,
in which the young Doinel (last seen spying on his girl
friend in *Love at Twenty*) is discharged from the army.
Doinel walks out of prison alone, searching for the relationships so long denied him. For Truffaut, "languishing
in the prison of Dupleix in Paris. . . . a dozen of us in a
cell built for four," such a relationship arrived in the
form of Bazin:

> Hanging onto the bars, the privileged prisoner of the
> moment turned around and said: "Anyone here named
> Truffaut?" I turned over on my mattress and heard: "Come
> look; your parents are here asking for you." More dum-
> founded than glad, I hoisted myself up along the door and
> saw not my parents but the Bazins, Janine and Andre, who
> had been refused permission to visit me and had hit upon
> the idea of opening a window along a stairway and shouting
> my name.[8]

It was Bazin's persistence that finally led to Truffaut's
discharge, the second time the French intellectual critic
had rescued this as yet unproven creative talent. Without
Bazin Truffaut might have languished longer in jail and
finally drifted down into the bitter depths of French
society. Instead, he began writing on film, joining a group
of young writers who shared with him an enthusiasm for
cinema that bordered on religious fervor. Andre Bazin
was their spiritual leader, opening doors for them to
write, especially through *Cahiers du Cinema*, which under
Bazin's direction became one of the world's leading film
publications. Bazin and his young writer-friends were in

7. *L'Express* interview.
8. From a memoir to Bazin, published in *Cahiers du Cinema*, January,
1959.

some respects sharply different. Truffaut, in particular, attacked filmmakers he disliked, lashing out with such appraisals as this about one director: "He is outrageous, he goes much too far. His film is stupefyingly malicious. It is venom spat out as generously as hemoglobin."[9] Bazin objected to such intemperate attacks. He himself was a shy and frail man, and when critics were too vigorous in their attacks, "he would defend not the filmmaker or the journalist, but the man, in a plea on his behalf that was always generous and intelligent. . . . He gave everybody a chance."[10] As a critic Truffaut soon focused on a major concern, the development of the *politique des auteurs* (policy of authors), the critical approach that evaluates film by authorship, which is to say, by the individual creative personality behind the film, namely the director. Any director who managed to rise above the studio system and place his personal stamp on the films he directed was embraced as an *auteur*— sometimes, unfortunately, when his work was mediocre. In rebellion against the Hollywood studio system, which he felt stifled creativity, Truffaut stated blatantly that "cinema cannot be an art so long as it is the result of the work of a group."[11] He and his fellow *auteur* critics, all of whom had grown up watching the Hollywood films of the thirties and forties, as well as the French pictures of the same era, took delight in locating obscure directors who were victims of the oppressive studio system but who nevertheless were able, in "formula" and B films, to establish their own style and place a distinctive personal signature on their films. Thus, an American director like Samuel Fuller—unknown in American critical circles—was designated an *auteur* because such pictures as *I Shot Jesse James* and *Merrill's Marauders* are so clearly the work of a single artist in command of his particular medium. Andrew Sarris, the American critic who has been so

9. Reprinted in the Grove Press edition of *The 400 Blows*, p. 222.
10. Truffaut in *Cahiers du Cinema*, January, 1959.
11. *Cahiers du Cinema*, p. 221.

influential on this side of the Atlantic in applying the *auteur* approach to criticism, examines American directors by categories, beginning with the true *auteurs*—Ford, Chaplin, Griffith, Hawks, and others—and working down to the lower levels of directors he considers "one-shots" or guilty of "strained seriousness."

More must be said about the *auteur* approach to criticism, but for the moment I mention it to suggest Truffaut's beginning as a theoretician who reflects the same concern for serious study of cinema that characterized Bazin. To examine the underlying vision reflected in Truffaut's own films, we must approach that vision first through an analysis of Bazin's understanding of film, and then in terms of the *politique des auteurs*.

2

Andre Bazin

The richness and versatility, the mystical and spiritual quality of Andre Bazin tempt me to devote more space than is possible here to an examination of his film aesthetics. What I propose to do here is to consider one aspect of Bazin's work, his careful distinction between those filmmakers who believe in *image* and those who believe in *reality*.[1] This distinction is crucial to our understanding of Truffaut, for as I read Truffaut's style, he clearly opts for the *reality*, rather than the *image*, approach to direction. With this in mind, let me state rather quickly just how Bazin uses those terms.

Consider for a moment that the original motion pictures in the 1900-1912 era were essentially photographed plays, the camera taking up a position front-row center and photographing all that occurred on stage. A major contribution of D. W. Griffith—though by no means his only contribution—was the development of film-editing from a simple pasting together of scenes to a skillful manipulation of images in such a way that a feeling beyond the scenes themselves was conveyed to the audience. It seems elementary to us now, but Griffith perfected the rescue sequence, with the brave men riding on their horses to the rescue of the frightened damsel who is

1. Bazin discusses these terms in an essay that appears in at least two English translations, one in *What Is Cinema?* and the other in *The New Wave*, edited by Peter Graham (New York: Doubleday, 1968).

besieged in a cabin, a fort, or a house. Griffith cut back and forth between the rider and the lady in distress, creating in the audience a feeling of suspense as he made the images of rescuer and rescuee shorter and shorter until the dramatic moment when the two came together in a final embrace. This process of cutting back and forth is termed "parallel editing" and consists of reporting on two separate events but linking them in a significant manner.

It remained for Russian film directors like Sergei Eisenstein and Vsevolod Pudovkin to develop editing into what came to be called "montage," the creating of a greater reality out of the combination of two or more other realities. Or, to use Bazin's more precise definition, montage is "the creation of a sense of meaning not proper to the images themselves but derived exclusively from their juxtaposition."[2] One form of montage that was used effectively in the twenties—though it is no longer used, possibly because it is too blatantly obvious for the contemporary viewer—is what Bazin refers to as "montage by attraction." In Pudovkin's film *Mother* (1927), the Russian director showed a crowd of workers marching down the street, and then cut immediately to a picture of an ice flow, suggesting that the women were marching down the street with the same relentless pressure as ice flowing down a river. The introduction of such an obvious symbol today would be considered overdrawn, but in the early days of montage it was highly effective.

Montage remains the basic principle of editing, however—that is, for those filmmakers who, as Bazin suggests, put their faith in image rather than reality. Every film student is familiar with the famous experiment Lev Kulesnov conducted with Pudovkin, in which a Russian actor was photographed in three similar closeups, expressing no particular emotion. The facial closeups were then joined with three separate bits of film, one showing a

2. *What Is Cinema?*, p. 25.

plate of soup standing on a table, another a coffin with a dead woman, and the third a little girl playing with a toy bear. In a book on editing, Podovkin comments:

> When we showed the three combinations to an audience which had not been let into the secret, the result was terrific. They pointed out the heavy pensiveness of his mood over the forgotten soup, were touched and moved by the deep sorrow with which he looked on the dead woman, and admired the light, happy smile with which he surveyed the girl at play. But we knew in all three cases the face was exactly the same.[3]

This, in brief, is the meaning of montage, the creating of a reality that is more than the sum of the parts presented. Now I have not meant to imply that there is such a thing as a film without montage, or at least without editing. Except for an Andy Warhol-type film that runs continuously looking at the same subject (a man sleeping or the Empire State Building), all films have some editing. But it is the stylist who "believes in," or "has faith in," the montage who is to be distinguished from the director who puts primary emphasis on reality.

A second category emphasizing image rather than reality Bazin calls "plastics," by which he means "the style of the sets, of the make-up, and performers." In addition, "plastics" involves lighting and the framing of a shot. Lest the reader despair over the use of terms like "plastics" and "montage" to describe film styles that are foreign to him, let me say that the important thing is to grasp the essence of Bazin's distinctions. We must not get hung up on the terms he uses to make these distinctions. So to repeat, the director who puts his greater faith in image is the director who will make great use of montage and plastics to impose an order and a "look" on his subject. I have stressed this style at the outset because this is the traditional cinema, the Hollywood movie, in

3. *Film Technique and Acting* (Hackensack, N.J.: Wehman), p. 140.

which the director creates with his editing and his arrangement of scenes something that he wishes the viewer to experience. Bazin sums it up: "Through the contents of the image and the resources of montage, the cinema has at its disposal a whole arsenal of means whereby to impose its interpretation of an event on the spectator."[4]

I have tried to suggest that the style of directing that emphasizes image is a valid style, that in fact some sort of editing is of the essence of film making and is what originally makes film different from staged drama. A viewing of D. W. Griffith's *Birth of a Nation* will indicate something of the power of ordering what is photographed in such fashion as to create significant reactions in the viewer.

But simultaneously with the image directors there have been other artists who used the camera in a different way. These are the artists whose major concern is not the creation of images, but the evocation of reality. Bazin suggests that Erich von Stroheim, F. W. Murnau, and Robert Flaherty—silent film directors working originally in the 1920s—made very little use of montage. In *Nanook of the North*, for example, Flaherty could have suggested through montage the period of waiting as Nanook hunted the seal. He chose instead to show the actual waiting period, for the length of the hunt itself is the "very substance of the image, its true object."[5] Or again, Murnau is not trying to be impressionistic in the images he presents in *Nosferatu*, for to do so would be to deliberately frame his subject so as to create a reaction in the viewer. Rather, Murnau lets his camera reveal the "structural depth" of the subject at hand. He does not put together the reality, he allows it to reveal itself. The same is true of von Stroheim's *Blind Husbands* and *Foolish Wives*, harsh portrayals of the decadent upper class in the early 1920s. Bazin reminds us that von Stroheim has

4. *What Is Cinema?*, p. 26.
5. *What Is Cinema?*, p. 27.

one simple rule for direction: "Take a close look at the
world, keep on doing so, and in the end it will lay bare
for you all its cruelty and its ugliness."[6] All three of
these artists are concerned not to provide an image that
adds to reality, but to allow reality to reveal itself.

I have spent considerable time allowing Bazin to reveal
himself in his perceptive distinction between two styles
of filmmakers in order to suggest that the potency of
Truffaut's work lies precisely in the fact that he allows
his films to reveal what is present in the material under
consideration. This does not mean, of course, that such
work is undertaken with a camera staring blindly at any
scene. An artist like Flaherty or Truffaut has a clear
understanding of what he wishes to present to an audience, and he selects the material he will photograph to
present his personal vision. He orders his material according to his personal vision, and he photographs it to suit
that vision. But the important thing is that his style of
work is concerned with capturing reality, evoking the
presence of an Eskimo igloo or a Paris courtyard. He does
this not by cutting from one part of the igloo or courtyard to another, but by carefully examining, by probing,
with the camera to allow the igloo or courtyard to
happen.

Bazin's distinction, I must repeat, is not intended to
suggest that a filmmaker like Truffaut has no interest in
montage or plastics. The scene early in *Jules and Jim* in
which Catherine first meets the two men is a masterful
montage, showing Catherine walking down the stairs and
then cutting in quickly with shots revealing that she looks
like a statue the men have admired and sought. This is
montage, and Truffaut uses it effectively to say much
more about Catherine than is immediately present in a
single closeup of her face. Such early sequences as when
Catherine's nightgown catches fire or when the three
have a footrace also involve montage. But I would suggest

6. *What Is Cinema?*, p. 27.

that Truffaut uses the montage effect to create a world quickly, a world in which two men love the same woman. Once this world has been created, set forth rapidly so that the viewer has no time to object to the unconventional nature of their relationship, then Truffaut can slow down and concentrate on the reality he has created. The dominant motif of his work is to focus on the reality of the image, allowing it to reveal itself. As the film draws to a conclusion, however, and Catherine prepares to take Jim to death over the end of the bridge, the montage effect is reintroduced, again in order to create a fantasy world which will permit the artist to conclude this examination of a world that the viewer would normally reject.

Consider the beautifully framed shot of Catherine, Jules, and Jim emerging from separate windows in their "handsome, white-painted house" in the south of France. We first see the house in medium closeup with all the shutters closed. The facade is bathed in sunlight. Catherine appears at the center window on the first floor, calling for Jules, who is picked up by a rapid pan as he emerges from a window on the same floor. Then, without a cut, the camera pans upwards to reveal Jim emerging from a top-floor window. They exchange pleasantries and Jules announces that they are going to the beach. In sharp contrast to the rapid editing that has characterized the events before they reach the white house, the next scene emerges in a slow dissolve, picking up the threesome as they walk through the woods, heading for a swim. The camera tracks through the woods, picking up little bits of debris left behind, suggesting that others have found joy in this setting. They climb a tree, and the camera scans the horizon, picking out the white house in the distance. Truffaut repeats some of this same forest exploration in his more recent *The Wild Child,* allowing the camera to examine the habitat of the child until it reveals itself as deep, silent, and threatening.

Had Truffaut opened *Jules and Jim* at this leisurely pace, his audience would have rejected this strange trio as unreal. It is only after he has created their reality through montage that he dares slow down and let us live with them in the caressing camera pans that take in the idyllic settings they occupy before the inevitable doomed ending is taken up with a return to the rapid montage.

At this point we must examine in more detail just how the language of the cinema handles the matter of photographing reality, lest the reader assume we are talking about *cinema verité*, or the kind of reality that the television cameraman picks up walking down a riot-torn city street. Great care is taken to pick up precisely the reality the director seeks to have revealed. But the director does not manipulate interest by cutting. Rather he shoots all the relevant items in a single frame (using "depth of focus" so as not to control interest by focus) and creates his emphases by the placement of the elements within the frame. Truffaut could have utilized montage to give us the first glimpse of the *ménage à trois* in the white house, cutting from a medium shot of the house to closeups of the three principals emerging from their respective windows. But this would have said to the audience, "Look, one by one the trio emerges from the house, so you know they are living here together." There would have been a deliberate comment on the trio living together, an emphasis that would have left no doubt that the director felt a certain way about the arrangement. Or, as Bazin puts it, "Montage by its very nature rules out ambiguity of expression." But by including all elements in the same frame, Truffaut injects ambiguity. He lets the scene reveal itself, making no immediate comment on the living arrangement but letting the full-frame revelation speak rather positively of their situation because it seems kind of jolly to have each one occupy his own cozy little room in the white house in the south of France. At the same time, they *are* living in the same house, and so the viewer is caught with ambiguous reactions, enjoying the revelation given him in the frame, but also a little disconcerted over that revelation. A montage shot of the same setting would, as I have suggested, leave no doubt as to the director's attitude toward the trio, in part perhaps because closeups of facial expressions might seem to leer. The important thing is to note the difference between the use of montage and the portrayal of reality within a single frame.

By working with film as "reality" a filmmaker may use "depth of focus," the examination of several ingredients in the same frame. By allowing elements in both foreground and background to remain in focus at the same time, the director permits the elements to interact with one another. He does not impose a meaning on the interaction because the interaction reveals itself. Consider the scene Andre Bazin points to in William Wyler's *The Best Years of Our Lives*. Here a paraplegic veteran is being married to his sweetheart in a living room. The couple stands to the right of the frame in the near foreground. Dana Andrews, serving as best man, stands to the left in the immediate foreground. Between Andrews and the couple, in sharp focus but in the background, stands his estranged wife, Teresa Wright. The audience is invited, of course, to participate in the happy wedding event, but Wyler would also have us aware that Andrews and his wife are very conscious of one another, a consciousness that takes place in the context of a wedding. The implication (and what actually does happen) is that they will come together again. This could have been shot in montage, cutting from face to face in the wedding scene to tell the audience that the couple will overcome their estrangement. But to have done this would have been to rather explicitly state to the audience what will happen to the couple. Instead, Wyler presents the entire ambiguous situation, in which the audience can discover for itself the possibility of reunion while at the same time fully experiencing the couple's estrangement. Wyler still controls audience reaction, but he does so with a different style than montage. Now Wyler's work is of a different order from Truffaut's because his hand is much heavier as he tells a story, but the important point here is that both men utilize a style that does not resort to montage to create a reality, but presents reality in its total context.

Truffaut explains this difference between montage and the single frame in a discussion of the shooting of *Fahrenheit 451.*

Films in which people tell lies are more difficult to put on the screen than those in which they tell the truth. At any rate, a lying scene requires twice as many shots as a straight scene. Here's an imaginary example. A good girl, pure and honest, says to her mum: "Mama, I am going to get married." The mother, sweet and loving, says: "Oh, my darling, how happy I am for you!" There is no earthly reason why that scene should not be done in one shot with both women in picture throughout. Now, if the girl were a little tart who is going to marry the man her mother is in love with; or yet again a fine, Snow White-type girl whose mother is an "Ugly Duchess," one has to break the scene down into five or six shots in such a way as *to give the audience information it will not get from the characters themselves.* (Italics mine)[7]

Montage is utilized to provide data not immediately available to the viewer, to emphasize (or even to distort) material the director wants the audience to receive.

    7. "Journal of Fahrenheit 451," *Cahiers du Cinema,* February-March, 1966, p. 14.

3

The New Wave

After Bazin came the New Wave. It could be said that Bazin made the New Wave possible and that he was its spiritual father. Of course, the New Wave is a complex critical topic all its own, and it would be impossible to develop in detail the controversy that has revolved around both the *auteur* theory and the New Wave directors who emerged out of the theory. But since Truffaut is an important member of the New Wave and since he is credited with having first written about the *auteur* theory as a critic, some reference to this general topic is in order before we examine in detail Truffaut's own films.

Andrew Sarris is the American critic who crossed the language barrier and brought the *auteur* theory to these shores. Writing in *Film Culture* in the winter of 1962-63, Sarris outlined the manner in which the French critics— Truffaut and others—described the *auteur* theory:

> The first premise of the *auteur* theory is the technical competence of a director as a criterion of value. . . . The second premise . . . is the distinguishable personality of the director. . . . The third and ultimate premise . . . is concerned with interior meaning . . . extrapolated from the tension between a director's personality and his material. . . .

The *auteur* theory is concerned with nothing less than a redirection of film criticism, developing criteria based on an individual director's total work, rather than on a

34

piecemeal examination of each film in terms of its impact
on an audience. Sarris' introduction of the *auteur* theory
to the American critical scene brought an immediate and
vigorous reaction from Pauline Kael, who saw in the
approach a celebration of "trash" (not dirty, but routine)
movies. Miss Kael's opposition was based on her own
critical approach, according to which she prefers to examine movies in terms of how she enjoys each experience.
She resents the treatment of film in artistic terms, preferring to keep movies for the masses. Obviously, what
Sarris—and the French *auteur* critics—were after was the
recognition of film as an art form that had the same
possibility for personal expression as painting or music.
Miss Kael prefers to consider film in terms of content and
make-up; Mr. Sarris evaluates film from the standpoint of
the personality of the director and how that personality
manifests itself through a particular film's technique.

Like most arguments among specialists in a given field,
the finer points of the Kael-Sarris conflict are lost to the
nonspecialists. Since both are intellectuals in the very
best sense of that word, and since both write quite
seriously about film, it is not always easy to see exactly
how they differ in evaluating film. Suffice it to say at
this point that the major difference rests in Miss Kael's
rejection of an overarching unity of criticism and Mr.
Sarris' insistence that criticism must be approached with
a certain consistency, based on a director's personal
stance.

This consistency is rooted in an approach to film that,
as Sarris puts it, "is not so much a theory as an attitude, a
table of values that converts film history into directorial
autobiography."[1] In contrast to Miss Kael, who prefers
to look at film first of all from the point of view of
subject matter, Sarris considers film in terms of the
director's technique, personal vision, and overall corpus.
He could find joy, for example, in tracing a directorial

1. *American Cinema* (New York: Dutton, 1969), p. 30.

touch from one film to another. Some critics would be bored by seeing a Howard Hawks picture that repeats the same basic Western plot. But Sarris finds pleasure in reporting that similarities exist between Hawks' *Rio Lobo* and *El Dorado*. What this means, of course, as Sarris notes, is that "the auteur critic risks the resentment of the reader by constantly judging the present in terms of the past."[2] Sarris approaches film in this manner as a regular critic for the *Village Voice*, a New York weekly, and he remains one of the leading critics in this country, as does Miss Kael, who writes a regular film column for *The New Yorker*.

Sarris' 1962 article on *auteur* criticism followed by six years Truffaut's first article on the subject in *Cahiers du Cinema*, January, 1954. At first, Truffaut referred to this critical theory as a way of supporting some directors and rejecting others. Thus, the worst films of some directors (like Jean Renoir) were perforce better, in his judgment, than the best films of other directors (like John Huston). In the late 1950s, this blind loyalty to some directors led to shallow criticism, the kind of limited vision that might lead literary critics to endorse every book Hemingway wrote simply because he wrote it, discovering, for example, merit in a failure like *Across the River and Into the Trees* simply because it was, after all, clearly recognizable as a Hemingway book despite its poor quality. Truffaut and his fellow critics for *Cahiers du Cinema* were in part reacting against a certain classical directing style in French films, as well as against the stifling atmosphere of the American studio system. They reasoned that if an obscure director like Sam Fuller could put his personal "signature" on a war film like *Merrill's Marauders*, he had to be an author—*auteur*—because he had made his personal statement against the tension of the oppressive studio bosses.

But this was the excess of the *auteur* theory. Its very

2. *American Cinema*, p. 33.

real merit lay in its call to critics and students of film to accept film as an art form with artists who worked to create their own personal visions on celluloid. Many American directors are still laboring under producers and studios as production-line laborers, grinding out a product with little, if any, personal style in the end result. These are not *auteurs*; they are craftsmen displaying greater or lesser talent as journeymen directors.

The *auteurs* who made the most distinctive mark on the world film scene, the *auteurs* who made the theory come alive with truly personal cinematic statements, were those French directors who were identified under the heading "The New Wave." As Peter Graham is quick to point out in the book he edited on the New Wave, it was less a "movement than a useful journalistic catchphrase; under it, a very heterogeneous bunch of film-makers were lumped together, some of them readily, but most of them willy-nilly."[3] What they did hold in common was an understanding of cinema as an art form that should be utilized for personal statements. Most were critics and thus articulate writers; and what is extremely important to building a "movement," they had their own journal, *Cahiers du Cinema,* as an outlet for their theories and arguments.

Truffaut's *The 400 Blows* was one of the first films made by a New Wave director. Jean Luc Godard's *Breathless* was another. These and other early New Wave films had several significant things in common: they were personal, they were made for very little money, allowing them to be personal, and they made nice profits. The fact that a personal, small-budget film could make money encouraged producers and investors to assist other young directors to make similar films, a phenomenon that was repeated in the United States when *Easy Rider,* which was made for under a million dollars in 1969, grossed many times that amount.

3. *The New Wave,* p. 7.

Among the directors emerging in that early stage of the New Wave in 1958-59 were Godard, Truffaut, Claude Chabrol, Jacques Rivette, and Eric Rohmer. Also related to the New Wave are Alain Resnais, Roger Vadim, Louis Malle, and Georges Franju. After a decade, these men have taken their place as established directors in French cinema with widely different styles. Most of them—especially Chabrol, Truffaut, Resnais, Godard, and Rohmer—can be depended upon to make personal films, quickly recognizable by their own unique style. And of all the critics-turned-filmmakers, no one has a more distinctive and consistent style than François Truffaut, whose films are the very best argument available for the viability of the *auteur* theory.

4

The Films

Truffaut's films through the summer of 1973 can be summed up in three categories: The Early Days; the leveling off of The Middle Period; and the return of Antoine Doinel in The Mature Truffaut.

In The Early Days, Truffaut made three pictures, two of which were critical and commercial successes in France and have since become classics in the United States. The first is the highly autobiographical *400 Blows*, which we have already discussed in our account of Truffaut's early life. The second picture, considered by Truffaut himself a work that shows his stumbling efforts to make a second film, is *Shoot the Piano Player*, virtually an homage to the American gangster genre. The third film, also discussed in detail earlier, is *Jules and Jim*. In my judgment this is Truffaut's best film, if by "best" I am allowed to mean a film in which he seems to be in almost total control of his medium as he projects the vision he wishes to share with his viewer.

In The Middle Years, which cover roughly 1956 to 1968, Truffaut had what must be considered a decline in creativity, a time in which he seemed to be searching for the right format for his vision. *Soft Skin* in 1964 was followed by *Fahrenheit 451* in 1966 and by his most overt homage to Hitchcock, *The Bride Wore Black*, in 1968.

The Mature Truffaut, working after 1968, clearly recovered the sensitivity of the early years, beginning with *Stolen Kisses* in 1968, followed by *Mississippi Mermaid* in 1969, *The Wild Child* and *Bed and Board* in 1970. His eleventh feature, *Two English Girls*, is based on a novel by Henri-Pierre Roche, who also wrote the novel from which Truffaut made *Jules and Jim*. Like *Jules and Jim* it has an early twentieth-century setting, though also like *Jules and Jim* it reflects very much the Truffaut vision of the 1970s.

To complete the Truffaut filmography, we shall mention his first short, *Les Mistons (The Mischief-makers)*, which was released in 1958, one year before his first feature. This is a good short film (twenty-six minutes) to use as an introduction to the Truffaut style. In 1962, Truffaut made an episode which is a part of his longer film *Love at Twenty*. This segment is titled *Antoine and Colette*, and represents an interim report on Antoine Doinel between his teen years in *The 400 Blows* and his courtship in *Stolen Kisses*.

It is in the mature Truffaut years that we find the Antoine Doinel story revealing the highly personal vision that Truffaut wants to share with his audiences. It is most unusual for a commercial feature film to self-consciously refer to a film other than itself, because to do so is to assume that the audience watching the second film has already seen the first. A novelist can afford this luxury, but feature filmmakers have usually treated each of their works as separate entities thrust out before the great paying public. One example of a Truffaut cross-reference appears in *Bed and Board*, the picture in which Antoine Doinel, played here as always by the same young actor Truffaut used in *The 400 Blows*, Jean-Pierre Leaud, is married to the girl he courted in *Stolen Kisses*. At one point in *Bed and Board*, Antoine and his wife Christine are having dinner with her parents and they go into the basement to select a dinner wine. Christine suddenly pushes her husband against the wall for a brief kiss. He responds in a husbandly fashion, tolerantly, with no enthusiasm. This scene is enriched for viewers who know that in *Stolen Kisses* Antoine followed Christine, then his sweetheart, into this same basement also to select dinner wine. While there he had stolen a kiss, brushing her against the wall of the basement. In linking these two scenes, before and after marriage, Truffaut makes the soft, gentle note that marriage has a way of changing a man's attitude toward stolen kisses.

Again, during *Stolen Kisses*, Antoine is hurrying across a city street when he encounters an old girl friend, accompanied by her husband and a small baby. He greets the couple with the sort of tolerant, strained attitude a shy man might evidence upon seeing a girl he once courted but did not marry. For the viewer seeing only *Stolen Kisses* in the Truffaut corpus, the scene is meaningful on one level, but the viewer who has also seen *Antoine and Colette,* the segment from *Love at Twenty,* recognizes the old girl friend as Colette. This recognition adds a certain poignancy to the chance encounter.

Throughout Truffaut's work there is an obvious preoccupation with the written word. He likes to use voice-over narrators reading from a diary *(The Wild Child)* or from a novel *(Jules and Jim* or *Two English Girls).* And he has a particular penchant for written correspondence. In *Jules and Jim,* letters cross each other in the mails, creating plot complications. In *Two English Girls,* Claude conducts a romance of sorts with Muriel and Anne by sending letters across the English Channel, and Claude's insights into his feelings for the two girls are communicated by mail to his mother in France. Or again, Truffaut uses the mails to unveil the shy insecurity of his hero in *Stolen Kisses,* when he follows in documentary style a letter mailed to the young man after he has fled in flustered embarrassment from the apartment of the shoe store owner.

In *Bed and Board* Truffaut hints that he has been "writing" his own life story through his films in the dialogue in which Jean-Pierre Leaud admits that he has been writing a novel. And of course, *Jules and Jim* and *Two English Girls* are both based on the only two novels written by Henri-Pierre Roche and both are set in that romantic early twentieth-century era when deepest emotions were shared in the mails, and not by telephone or in trysts set up by jet trips.

Stolen Kisses and *Bed and Board* offer another effective cross-reference. At various points in *Stolen Kisses*, a mysterious man is seen following Christine, each appearance accompanied by background music signaling uncertainty and possible danger. At the film's conclusion, the man approaches Antoine and Christine to announce his love for her and his desire to continue to admire her. There is really no point to his profession of love; it is just a small touch Truffaut adds to his total picture. In *Bed and Board*, on the other hand, when he allows a mysterious man to enter the film on several occasions, again accompanied by music suggesting danger, Truffaut is engaging in self-parody of his own earlier film. Just as the audience begins to anticipate that the man will provide another perplexing addition to the plot, he ceases to be a mysterious figure and is shown as a television performer on a variety show. The neighbors all gather about him the next time he comes into the courtyard and talk about their enjoyment of his TV performance. Again, there is no point to either his first appearances or this revelation. Truffaut is suggesting that life is filled with inconsequential events and that to live is to be exposed to these events.

This is why things do not "happen" to Truffaut's characters in ways that advance the film's plot or hold the audience in suspense. Rather, Truffaut's characters are revealed as living quietly, bumping into friends and having minor difficulties but generally making it through life as human beings operating with no more or no fewer limitations than anyone else. When plot events do occur, Truffaut emphasizes their irrelevance so as to make sure the viewer knows that when plot-line is manipulated it is done in an unreal way in order to tell the viewer a story. Truffaut is suggesting that life is not a plot to be described, but an existence to be revealed. In *Mississippi Mermaid,* for example, the revelation of the film is the gentle love Catherine Deneuve has for her husband. The plot, however, is melodramatic, following the wife as she deceives a plantation owner into marrying her and then on through to a climax when the wife tries to kill her husband with rat poison. Truffaut is suggesting to his viewers that film plots are not to be taken seriously since they are illusions *about* life. The things to take seriously are the things having to do with *real* existence. It is his desire to present real existence to his viewers through the unreal plot developments. But to make certain the viewer won't forget and start taking the plot about life seriously, Truffaut deliberately overdoes or undercuts his plot in such a way that he is saying to the viewer, "Look, you are watching a movie *about* life; this is not life itself." In this process, however, he is presenting life itself as a personal artistic vision which he very much wishes to share with the viewer.

The method Truffaut is using is referred to in literary criticism as irony. Writing about "The Literary Sophistication of François Truffaut" in a 1965 article in *Film Comment,* Michael Klein discusses irony as the use of language that deliberately undercuts itself. Evaluating the early years of Truffaut, Klein suggests that in both *Shoot the Piano Player* and *Jules and Jim* Truffaut relies on the techniques of dislocation and irony to impart his special vision to his viewers. By "dislocation" Klein means the deliberate manipulation of a work of art in order to snare the viewer into the frame of reference the artist wants him to share. "He may fragment the narrative, use an unreliable narrator, distort space, alter the temporal sequence, etc., to this rhetorical end. The dislocated reader or viewer, confused by distortions in the narrative, has to accept the author's view in order to make sense out of the material."[1]

Truffaut works within familiar genres—love stories, gangster films, murder mysteries—and manipulates audience response by dislocation in order to project his personal vision through these genres. In my discussion of Bazin's image-reality division of directors, I indicated that the image-oriented director creates a world through montage while the reality director allows a world to emerge through revelation. In *Jules and Jim* and *Shoot the Piano Player*, Truffaut creates a world through image technique, but he also creates a world of his own making through an ironical treatment and handling of familiar genres in realistic fashion. His irony allows him to be a realistic director, but still tightly control the audiences' reactions.

After Catherine's miscarriage, *Jules and Jim* shifts its lyrical style back to the fast-editing style of the beginning of the picture. There is a sense in which Truffaut is telling the audience that reality has ended. He will now terminate his film with the same kind of frantic fantasy found in the opening section. When Jim tells Catherine that he will not marry her, she suddenly pulls out a gun and threatens to kill him. He grabs her hand and after throwing down the gun leaps from the window and escapes. It is only a few minutes later (in film-time) that Catherine does succeed in killing Jim by driving over the bridge.

One director who has strongly influenced Truffaut is Jean Renoir. In his *Rules of the Game*, Renoir is busy sharing a comedy with his viewers. Suddenly, a chase ends with a gunshot, and it appears for the moment that someone has been killed. This dislocation keeps the audience upset, preventing it from settling down into set patterns of reaction. It is this dislocation that allows Renoir, and now Truffaut, to control the audience. The director calls the shots by determining what will be undercut in his material and in what way. Familiar reac-

1. *Film Comment*, Summer 1965, p. 24.

tions are no longer permitted. Audience involvement becomes imperative. Discussing the surprising suicide of Charlie's wife in *Shoot the Piano Player*, a film that parodies the gangster genre, Michael Klein points out that the suicide is an

> excellent parody of something that, with variations, has been done so many times. However, ironically, it isn't what we expected. The suicide gives us a jolt and we view the problems raised as serious. In short, Truffaut has rendered a cliché by parodying it. He has made us respond to a situation that, portrayed in a straightforward consistent manner, would have been dismissed easily.[2]

This technique allows Truffaut's films to be both "extremely funny and extremely serious." By parodying a cliché, Truffaut makes Charlie not just "the conventional Alger hero or the conventional laconic loner made funny. He is also a person to whom we respond with sympathy and horror."[3] What a marvelous way to allow a commercial medium to project a personal vision! Because audience expectations have been developed over a fifty-year period, Truffaut insists on keeping his audience off guard, dislocating it until he is allowed to have his personal say.

Truffaut is thus a master at handling reality because with his command of the film medium he is a master at handling ambiguity. It was Bazin who suggested that the image directors do not try to handle ambiguity. They manipulate material to make a specific point with their montage. The reality directors, on the other hand, examine a total scene with deep focus and suggest to the viewer that there are several layers of significance awaiting his consideration. Truffaut does not rely on deep focus within a frame, but he does project ambiguity through the use of irony. A student of mine once responded to a question I asked about *Jules and Jim* by commenting that she liked Catherine in spite of the fact

2. *Film Comment*, Summer 1965.
3. *Film Comment*, p. 26.

that a woman borders on the demonic. Now how is it possible to like someone who is unfaithful to both men in the film—men to whom the viewers have become very attached—and finally kills one of them? It is possible because Truffaut's ironical use of film establishes Catherine's complete personality in such a way that the viewer sees her in both her demonic nature and her desirable nature. In the footrace across the bridge, Catherine wins because she cheats. The background music is gay, and the spirit of the moment is one of good fun. The two men don't mind losing the race; it is not something to be taken seriously. But the fact that Catherine cheats does suggest, ever so gently, that there is trouble ahead in this relationship. Or to take another example, when Catherine leaps into the river, she does so to punish Jules for his failure to stand up for her. This motivation is trivial, and the jump has about it a spirit of compulsive freedom. But there is also a grimness about the experience—suggested by the narrator, undergirded by the background music, yet quickly relieved by the joyful scenes that follow.

Catherine, then, is not a psychological study of one woman. If she were, we would find her psychotic. Rather, Catherine is an artistic rendering of Truffaut's vision of humanity as ambiguous—on the one hand joyously creative and loving, and on the other, demonically murderous. Truffaut is perhaps more successful in rendering this totality in his presentation of Catherine Deneuve as the wife in *Mississippi Mermaid* who deceives her husband and then tries to poison him. Miss Deneuve is not as strong a personality as Jeanne Moreau, and it may be that she fits better as the female character into whom Truffaut can pour his understanding of ambiguity. She has the kind of passivity that also characterizes Jean-Pierre Leaud, whereas Miss Moreau is such a dominant personality that Truffaut has difficulty in keeping her personality from overriding his delicate sense of irony. In *Jules and Jim,* he kept Miss Moreau moving so rapidly that in contrast to the gentle, long-suffering Jules, and the passive Jim, she came across as both desirable and demonic. Some viewers, however, professed not to see anything desirable about her, finding instead the demonic as the dominant note. The gay music and impressionistic lighting were meant to create a positive attitude toward her, but these came close to failing because Miss Moreau is not an easy person to dominate, even with bright sunlight and gay music. I personally think Truffaut succeeded in keeping her under control, but he has an easier time of it with the passive Miss Deneuve in *Mississippi Mermaid*.

Truffaut was not so fortunate with Miss Moreau in *The Bride Wore Black*, a largely unsuccessful film which has her in the title role as a bride whose husband is murdered as they emerge from the church on the day of their wedding. Using a cliché plot, Truffaut has the bride track down all the men who were involved in the murder (it was a random shot taken during a poker game and was not intentional). She systematically kills each man, and while Truffaut succeeds in keeping the audience from being disturbed over the murders—he is here following Hitchcock—he does not succeed in projecting his vision of ambiguity. By setting up the movie-type plot, Truffaut worked against his true nature, leading one writer to describe both *The Bride Wore Black* and *Fahrenheit 451* as unsatisfactory because Truffaut was "working to some extent against his true self: decisions of the will were being allowed precedence over natural proclivities."[4]

Truffaut works most effectively, then, when his sense of irony is given full opportunity to operate. He shares his gentle vision with the viewers in the midst of a conventional context, which he in turn manipulates against the grain of the context itself. In short, Truffaut works best when he is showing how fragile a creature, yet how potent a power, is man. He might have been a

4. Robin Wood, "Chabrol and Truffaut," *Movie*, Winter 1969-70.

preacher and told us this in sermons, or he might have been an Ingmar Bergman and told us this in serious film studies of the silence of God. Instead, and this is because it is his nature to function this way, he presents his vision in the midst of quiet, little pictures that do nothing more than invite viewers to spend a little time with someone whose presence warms them by its honesty, openness, and finally by its willingness to present a whole vision that encompasses all aspects of man.

Even in Truffaut's reporting of the apparently trivial, he deals in profundity, a technique that reminds me of the style of John Updike's novels. Critics have been hounding Updike to write on major themes. He refuses, because he knows that by major themes these critics mean such things as war, peace, poverty, and race. He prefers to probe gently into what may be trivial on the surface, but what is in fact the most major theme of all—man and the human condition. Robin Wood sees a similarity to Renoir's handling of ambiguity in the manner in which Truffaut can take a single scene and demand that the viewer respond to many different experiences at once. He points to a scene in *Stolen Kisses*, for example, in which we are asked to react in the detective agency office "almost simultaneously to Antoine's female colleague trying on a wig, Antoine being fired for becoming the lover of a client's wife, and Monsieur Henri dying of a heart attack."[5]

It is not through montage that this simultaneity is established, but through pans and tracking shots, following the office activities, picking up action in the foreground and background, and finally focusing on the heart attack. When everyone rushes to the side of the stricken Henri, Truffaut has the amazing capacity to show consistent concern just by the mere presence of the office staff, gathered around the dead form of the colleague who moments before was very much in their midst. It is

5. *Movie*, p. 19.

simply in their quiet, concerned presence, rather than through what they say or through facial closeups, that the office force is presented as mankind-writ-large, a caring community. The death scene is followed immediately by the funeral, a sombre affair emphasizing in a more formal setting the grief already evidenced in a more meaningful manner through the gathering about the fallen man.

Following the funeral, Truffaut has Doinel go directly to a brothel, there to encounter a prostitute whom he treats with great consideration and respect. This unexpected and strange juxtapositioning reaffirms something the dead colleague Henri had told Doinel, a suggestion that the best cure for grief was love. But the irony of this event is that while Doinel has his own girl friend, he elects to go to a professional lover, where he will not receive love but where in an ironical fashion he is able to give a little compassion to his paid companion.

In The Early Years, Truffaut used music and montage to establish conditions for irony. The Mature Truffaut relies more on the soft understatement, the gesture, the unresolved tension within a scene, to maintain his irony. The Mature Truffaut is marked by restraint, reticence, and respect for the material under consideration.

In *Stolen Kisses*, for example, Antoine is employed by a shoe store owner to find out why his employees don't like him. It is obvious to the viewer that the owner is unpopular because he is insecure and overbearing, though in typical Truffaut fashion, he is not unpleasant. The employees do not really dislike him, they just don't like him. He is not explained, or developed; he is just there in his drabness. The viewer is invited to feel a bit uncomfortable in the lack of support he gets from his employees. But before we can become too concerned over the employer, Antoine himself commits a faux pas that sends him into total flight. Taking tea with his employer and his wife, Antoine is smitten by the wife's charm and beauty. As a result, shy and uncertain, he slips and refers to the wife as "sir" rather than "madame," sort of a "thank you sir" rather than a "thank you ma'm," if he had been speaking in English. Devastated by this error—from which anyone else would have quickly recovered—Antoine flees from the apartment, from the store, which is next door, and from his job. An overreaction? Of course, but an indication that Truffaut knows that what upsets the ordinary man is nothing to what can upset the sensitive soul. In order to display this added dimension of Antoine, a conventional director might have given us a conventional embarrassment—spilt tea, a broken zipper—but Truffaut uses a simple slip of the tongue, undercutting with irony the boy's need to flee and yet respecting the fact that for him this was a moment of intense humiliation. This is a superb handling of ambiguity. Mme. Tabard did not herself *cause* Antoine to call her "sir," and the event and the reaction come as quite a surprise to her. She is genuinely unprepared for what happens, just as the audience is unprepared. At the same time, the verbal slip was her fault because of who she is, a gracious and beautiful older woman. No one is condemned, no one is blamed. But all are involved, all are affected. This is the ambiguity of life. This is Truffaut.

By the standard of ambiguity, *The Wild Child* must be considered one of Truffaut's superior films. It is a documentary of an uncivilized being led into civilization, and Truffaut manages to leave the viewer with a recognition that civilization is at best a mixed blessing. The daring of this venture—Truffaut's first documentary—is emphasized by Truffaut's decision to play a major role himself in the film, his first venture in front of a camera.

The Wild Child offers convincing evidence that The Mature Truffaut has mastered his camera style and has control of his medium, allowing him to project his vision with a precision rarely found in commercial cinema today. In *The Wild Child*, he returns to work with a young actor, indicating again that he is not only a superior craftsman possessed of a clear vision, but also a sensitive and creative director of performers, and most especially boys of the age that Truffaut was when he first broke out of the convention of a drab home and entered the ambiguity of Paris society.

The Wild Child is adapted from a book by a Dr. Jean Itard, *Memoire et Rapport sur Victor de l'Aveyron*, written in 1806, which is a factual account of the civilization of a child who had lived in a forest, apparently as a wild beast, from around the age of three or four until his capture at about the age of twelve. The child cannot speak, and reacts in every way as a wild animal might react when captured by men. Dr. Itard persuades the authorities to let him train the child, and with the help of a motherly housekeeper, he sets up a pocket of civilization in his country home in order to gradually move the child from primitive savagery to normal human existence.

In the role of the child is Jean-Pierre Cargol, a gypsy boy Truffaut found in the south of France. Truffaut reports that he chose to play the role of Dr. Itard himself because as director he would have to guide the boy's performance and he thought that he might as well do so in front as well as behind the camera. The role of Dr. Itard is essentially that of the stiff, proper scientific man obsessed with abstraction and education. Perhaps Truffaut felt that as a non-actor, which he admittedly is, he could successfully convey the rational Dr. Itard better than any trained actor, who might be tempted to infuse a certain vitality into the role. What Truffaut was apparently after—and certainly what he got—was a Dr. Itard who in 1800 was the cold, impersonal man Stanley Kubrick gives us in 2001, deficient in feeling and devoted to reason. It would not be accurate, on the other hand, to say that Itard is completely devoid of feeling. He obviously cares for young Victor and desperately wants him to learn. But Truffaut, with his sensitivity to ambiguity, manages to suggest that while Itard wants the child to learn, he may be wishing for this more to advance a theory than to help the child.

Employing a documentary style, Truffaut follows the child's slow and difficult progress from a total inability to communicate to a gradual recognition of words and signs. Truffaut has said that he made his film in black and white—his first without color since *Jules and Jim*—because he wanted to create a tone of antiquity. He also employed some silent film techniques—notably an iris effect—in an effort to take the viewer backwards in time. As Truffaut pointed out in an interview, he knew that he could not create a nineteenth-century film technique since the first movies were made around 1900, but he did want to shove the viewer some distance away from 1970, and silent-film techniques would accomplish this. Referring to Pasolini's film *The Gospel According to St. Matthew,* he commented that he objected to Pasolini's use of a zoom lens in one shot because he thought while viewing the film, "They didn't have zoom lens in the first century!"

In *Jules and Jim,* Truffaut used rapid montage to create the slightly frantic, but giddy atmosphere of pre-World War I Europe. He creates an entirely different mood in *The Wild Child* with long, slow pans and leisurely looks at the pastoral scenery around the Itard home. It is Truffaut's film style that establishes the wildness of the boy's original forest home, providing the viewer an immediate entry into a world strange to 1970 eyes. Then when the child is brought to Itard's home, the neatness and the confinement of rooms and staircases is established by set shots that give the impression almost of a static drama being enacted within the four walls of the house.

The audience is anxious for the boy to succeed in his progress from forest to manor. And we struggle with Dr. Itard over every small step as the boy moves from an animalistic union with nature to a separation from nature into the world of abstraction, the world of words and principles. But there are moments that cause unease, a gentle suggestion by Truffaut that although Dr. Itard really had no choice but to lead the child into civilization, there is something quite sinister about removing this wild child from his close harmony with nature. In one memorable scene, the child is shown on the grass in front of the house, his face lifted to receive the wetness of the falling rain. He rolls about the grass in complete abandonment, momentarily at one again with the nature he has had to leave. At first the viewer considers this scene with the same mild pleasure as does Dr. Itard, accepting it as a childlike diversion from the more important assignment at hand, namely his education. But here is Truffaut's ambiguity at work again. Which, in fact, is more natural for the child, to unite with nature or to separate from nature with abstract symbols?

One way of seeing the sensitive ambiguity of *The Wild Child* is to compare it with a similar film Truffaut himself had hoped to make, *The Miracle Worker*. When this play about Helen Keller was first produced in Paris, Truffaut wired his agent in New York and asked him to secure the rights to film the play. The word came back that the rights had already been sold to Arthur Penn, who subsequently made the play into the award-winning film with Anne Bancroft and Patty Duke. Penn's film about the deaf-mute Miss Keller parallels *The Wild Child*, because the French savage was also closed off from civilization by his inability to communicate. But there is an important difference. *The Miracle Worker* never raises the question of whether it is well for Miss Keller to learn to communicate. It simply assumes that it is, and the film proceeds to the logical conclusion when she finally discovers the word for water. There is no ambiguity here, only the dramatic unfolding of a plot with which the audience is wholly sympathetic.

It is a measure of Truffaut's skill as a film artist that in *The Wild Child* he can actually create a world, a context, in which there is some room to doubt that the boy's best interests are served by his leaving the forest. Obviously, logic and reason point out that the child is not an animal but a human being, and that he is not equipped to live in the forest. But what Truffaut does in *The Wild Child* is to eschew this logic and create a fresh and open pastoral world in sharp juxtaposition to the confined world of the Itard house, thereby saying that within the created context of the film there is some room for ambiguity as to where the boy might find his fulfillment. Truffaut manipulates his audience into accepting his preconditions, and then presents the audience with an ambiguous reality within the context of that film. Argue with Truffaut's presuppositions, and you miss the force of his artistic vision. Argue with the morality of Catherine as she relates to Jules and Jim, and you miss the power of Truffaut. In the same way, consider *The Wild Child* as a victory for educational methodology and you fail to receive the deeper and more disturbing question Truffaut presents. The film closes on this note when the child, having run away from home, returns because he has already been conditioned away from wildness. Dr. Itard greets him with enthusiasm, saying, "My little Victor, you have come back to us by your own choice. You are no longer a savage, even if you are not yet a man. There is great hope for you." The child then turns and trudges slowly upstairs to bed, trailed by Dr. Itard's cheerful cry, "Soon we'll start our lessons again."

By now the reader is aware that Truffaut's prowess as an *auteur* director lies in a mastery of film style that is uniquely his own—though clearly influenced by the likes of Renoir and Hitchcock—and that he possesses a vision offering hope to a world that has difficulty seeing joy in the midst of ambiguity. Perhaps this study of Truffaut will encourage the reader to approach cinema in a more holistic manner, considering the various directors in terms of their total work and not just on the basis of one or two films. The American viewer whose sole exposure to Truffaut is limited to *Fahrenheit 451* would be unable to grasp the full measure of the man from that limited a viewing. Truffaut, like other directors who deserve the appellation of *auteur*, must be seen in his entirety to fully receive the potent and sensitive vision he shares.

Perhaps it takes a particular turn of mind and sensibility to gain the kind of pleasure the *auteur* critic experiences when he watches variations on a common theme appearing through an *auteur's* many films. But if there is pleasure in unity and connection, then there must be joy in finding the repeated scene worked gracefully in different films. I think, for example, of the first Truffaut short, *Les Mistons,* and the opening segment in which the young girl rides her bicycle happily through the streets and out into the countryside. This scene is repeated, with variations, as Catherine rides her bicycle through the countryside, trailed by both Jules and Jim, all of them dressed in white to accentuate the brightness of the sunlit day.

But there is more than simply the repetition of a scene from *Les Mistons* to *Jules and Jim.* An artist is sharing a vision with his viewer, and because he finds in the careful bicycle ride a symbol of a particular feeling he wishes to convey, he returns to this symbol when he wants to convey the same feeling in a later film. Or again, when Catherine, Jules, and Jim are temporarily lost in the woods near their home in the south of France, they climb a tree to see if they can gain their bearings. The camera pans across the horizon, peering through the forest, and finally finds the clearing through which the house appears, silent and white in the sun, waiting for the return of the three free spirits. Ten years later, in *The Wild Child,* Truffaut again pans across the horizon of a forest, looking through the branches and leaves, establishing a context of wildness and freedom, but undercutting this context immediately with the arrival of hunting dogs come to capture the wild child and bring him into the logic and security of civilization. A scene is repeated, a theme is restated, but in totally different settings. What matters is that an artist has said again what he said ten years earlier: Man's free spirit longs for the joy of the wild and unfettered forest, but his reason forces him to return to the more systematic patterns of civilization. Each of the two films says this, but to experience them both is to have the vision reiterated and reinforced. When the vision is as compelling and convincing as Truffaut's, it is a vision to experience over and over again.

Filmography

THE MISCHIEF-MAKERS (LES MISTONS); 1958. *Screenplay:* François Truffaut. Based on the short story "Virginales" by Maurice Pons. *Photography:* Jean Maligo. *Editor:* Cecile Decugis. *Music:* Maurice Le Roux. *Commentary:* Michel François. *Production:* Les Films du Carrosse. 26 minutes.

    Players: Bernadette LaFont (Bernadette), Gerard Blain (Gerard).

Rent from Pyramid Films, Box 1048, Santa Monica, Calif. 90406.

THE 400 BLOWS (LES QUATRE CENTS COUPS); 1959. *Screenplay:* François Truffaut. *Dialogue:* Marcel Moussy. *Story:* François Truffaut. *Photography:* Henri Decae. *Art Director:* Bernard Evein. *Editor:* Marie-Josephe Yoyotte. *Music:* Jean Constantin. *Sound:* Jean-Claude Marchetti. *Production:* Les Films du Carrosse/SEDIF. 94 minutes.

    Players: Jean-Pierre Leaud (Antoine Doinel), Clair Maurier (his mother), Albert Remy (his father), Guy Decomble (schoolmaster), Patrick Auffay (Rene), Georges Flamant (Rene's father), Daniel Couturier, François Nocher, Richard Kanayan (children). Special guest appearance by Jeanne Moreau (woman in street with dog) and Jean-Claude Brialy (man in street).

Rent from Janus Films, 745 Fifth Ave., New York, N.Y. 10022.

SHOOT THE PIANO-PLAYER (TIREZ SUR LE PIANISTE); 1960. *Screenplay:* François Truffaut, Marcel Moussy. *Dialogue:* François Truffaut. Based on the novel *Down There* by David Goodis. *Photography:* Raoul Coutard. *Art Director:* Jacques Mely. *Editor:* Claudine Bouche. *Music:* Jean Constantin. Song "Dialogues d'amoureux" composed and sung by Felix Leclerc and Lucianne Vernay. Song "Framboise" composed by Boby Lapointe. *Sound:*

Jacques Gallois. *Producer:* Pierre Braunberger. *Production:* Les Films de la Pleiade. 80 minutes.

Players: Charles Aznavour (Charlie Koller/Edouard Saroyan), Nicole Berger (Theresa), Marie Dubois (Lena), Michele Mercier (Clarisse), Albert Remy (Chico Saroyan), Claude Mansard (Momo), Daniel Boulanger (Ernest), Richard Kanayan (Fido Saroyan), Jacques Aslanian (Richard Saroyan), Serge Davri (Plyne), Claude Heymann (Lars Schmeel).
Rent from Janus Films, 745 Fifth Ave., New York, N.Y. 10022.

JULES AND JIM (JULES ET JIM); 1961. *Screenplay:* François Truffaut, Jean Grault. Based on the novel by Henri-Pierre Roche. *Photography:* Raoul Coutard. *Editor:* Claudine Bouche. *Music:* Georges Delerue. Song "Le Tourbillon" by Bassiak. *Sound:* Temoin. *Production:* Les Films du Carrosse/SEDIF. 105 minutes.

Players: Jeanne Moreau (Catherine), Oskar Werner (Jules), Henri Serre (Jim), Marie Dubois (Therese), Vanna Urbino (Gilberte), Sabine Haudepin (Sabine), Boris Bassiak (Albert), Michel Subor (Narrator).
Rent from Janus Films, 745 Fifth Ave., New York, N.Y. 10022

LOVE AT TWENTY (L'AMOUR A VINGT ANS; one episode in this film is ANTOINE ET COLETTE); 1962. *Screenplay:* François Truffaut. *Dialogue:* Yvon Samuel. *Photography:* Raoul Coutard. *Editor:* Claudine Bouche. *Linking Music:* Georges Delerue. *Producer:* Pierre Rostang. *Production:* Ulysse-Unitec.

Players: Jean-Pierre Leaud (Antoine Doinel), Marie-France Pisier (Colette), François Darbon (Colette's father), Rosy Varte (Colette's mother).

SOFT SKIN (LA PEAU DOUCE); 1964. *Screenplay:* François Truffaut, Jean-Louis Richard. *Photography:* Raoul Coutard. *Editor:* Claudine Bouche. *Music:* Georges Delerue. *Production:* Les Films du Carrosse/SEDIF. 118 minutes.

Players: Jean Desailly (Pierre Lachenay), Françoise Dorleac (Nicole Chomette), Nelly Benedetti (Franca Lachenay), Daniel Ceccaldi (Clement), Laurence Badie (Ingrid), Jean Lanier (Michel), Paule Emanuele (Odile), Philippe Dumat (cinema manager), Pierre Risch (Canon), Dominique Lacarriere (Pierre's secretary), Sabine Haudepin (Sabine), Maurice Garrel (bookseller), Gerard Poirot

(Franck), Georges de Givray (Nicole's father), Charles Lavialle (hotel night-porter), Carnero (Lisbon organizer), Catherine Duport (young girl at Reims dinner). Rent from Columbia Cinemateque, 711 Fifth Ave., New York, N.Y. 10022.

FAHRENHEIT 451; 1966. *Screenplay:* François Truffaut, Jean-Louis Richard. Based on the novel by Ray Bradbury. *Additional dialogue:* David Rudkin, Helen Scott. *Photography:* Nicolas Roeg. *Art Director:* Syd Cain. *Design and costume consultant:* Tony Walton. *Special effects:* Bowie Films, Rank Films Processing Division, Charles Staffel. *Editor:* Thom Noble. *Music:* Bernard Herrmann. *Sound:* Norman Wanstall. *Producer:* Lewis M. Allen. *Production:* Anglo-Enterprise/Vineyard. 112 minutes.

Players: Oskar Werner (Montag), Julie Christie (Linda Montag/Clarisse), Cyril Cusack (the captain), Anton Diffring (Fabian), Jeremy Spenser (man with the apple), Bee Duffell (the book-woman), Gillian Lewis (TV announcer), Ann Bell (Doris), Caroline Hunt (Helen), Anna Palk (Jackie), Roma Milne (neighbor). Rent from Universal 16, 221 Park Ave., South, New York, N.Y. 10003.

THE BRIDE WORE BLACK (LA MARIEE ETAIT EN NOIR); 1969. *Screenplay:* François Truffaut, Jean-Louis Richard. Based on the novel by Cornell Woolrich. *Photography:* Raoul Coutard. *Art Director:* Pierre Guffroy. *Editor:* Claudine Bouche. *Music:* Bernard Herrmann. *Sound:* Rene Levert. *Producer:* Marcel Roberts. *Production:* Les Films du Carrosse/Artistes Associes (Paris)/Dino de Laurentiis Cinematografica (Rome). 107 minutes.

Players: Jeanne Moreau (Julie Kohler), Jean-Claude Brialy (Corey), Michel Bouquet (Robert Coral), Charles Denner (Fergus), Claude Rich (Bliss), Daniel Boulanger (Delvaux), Michel Lonsdale (Clement Morane), Serbe Rousseau (David), Jazques Robiolles (Charlie), Luce Fabiole (Julie's mother). Rent from United Artists/16, 729 Seventh Ave., New York, N.Y. 10019.

STOLEN KISSES (BAISERS VOLES); 1968. *Screenplay:* François Truffaut, Claude de Givray, Bernard Revon. *Photography (Eastman Colour):* Denys Clerval. *Art Director:* Claude Pignot. *Editor:* Agnes Guillemot. *Music:* Antoine Duhamel. Song "Que reste-t-il de nos amours?" composed and sung by Charles Trenet. *Sound:* Rene Levert. *Producer:* Marcel Berbert. *Production:* Les Films du Carrosse/Artistes Associes. 91 minutes.

Players: Jean-Pierre Leaud (Antoine Doinel), Delphine Seyrig (Fabienne Tabard), Claude Jade (Christine Darbon), Michel Lonsdale (M. Tabard), Harry Max (M. Henri), Andre Falcon (M. Blady), Claire Duhamel (Mme. Darbon), Daniel Ceccaldi (M. Darbon), Paul Pavel (M. Julien), Serge Rousseau (the man), Martine Ferriere (manageress of the shoe shop), Catherine Lutz (Mme. Catherine), Simono (conjurer's friend), Roger Trapp (hotel manager), Jacques Delord (conjurer), Jacques Rispal (deceived husband), Martine Brochard (unfaithful wife), Robert Cambourakis (lover), Marie-France Pisier (Colette), Jean-François Adam (her husband).

Rent from United Artists/16, 729 Seventh Ave., New York, N.Y. 10019.

MISSISSIPPI MERMAID (LA SIRENE DU MISSISSIPPI); 1969. *Screenplay:* François Truffaut. Based on the novel *Waltz into Darkness* by William Irish. *Photography:* Denys Clerval. *Art Director:* Claude Pignot. *Editor:* Agnes Guillemot. *Music:* Antoine Duhamel. *Sound:* Rene Levert. *Producer:* Marcel Berbert. *Production:* Les Films du Carrosse/Artistes Associes/Produzioni Associate Delphos (Rome). 123 minutes.

Players: Jean-Paul Belmondo (Louis Mahe), Catherine Deneuve (Marion/Julie Roussel), Michel Bouquet (Comolli), Nelly Borgeaud (Berthe Roussel), Marcel Berbert (Jardine), Martine Ferriere (landlady), Roland Thenot (Richard).

Rent from United Artists/16, 729 Seventh Ave., New York, N.Y. 10019.

THE WILD CHILD (L'ENFANT SAUVAGE); 1970. *Screenplay:* François Truffaut, Jean Grault. Based on the book *Memoire et Rapport sur Victor de l'Aveyron* by Jean Itard. *Photography:* Nestor Almendros. *Art Director:* Jean Mandroux. *Editor:* Agnes Guillemot. *Sound:* Rene Levert. *Producer:* Marcel Berbert. *Production:* Les Films du Carrosse/Artistes Associes.

Players: Jean-Pierre Cargol (Victor, the "wild child"), Paul Ville (Remy), François Truffaut (Jean Itard), Françoise Seigner (Madame Guerin), Claude Miller (Monsieur Lemeri), Annie Miller (Madame Lemeri).

Rent from United Artists/16, 729 Seventh Ave., New York, N.Y. 10019.

BED AND BOARD (DOMICILE CONJUGAL); 1970. *Screenplay:* François Truffaut. *Players:* Jean-Pierre Leaud (Antoine Doinel), Claude Jade (Christine Doinel), Mille Hiroko (Kyoko). Rent from Columbia Cinemateque, 711 Fifth Ave., New York, N.Y. 10022.

TWO ENGLISH GIRLS; 1972. *Screenplay:* François Truffaut and Jean Grault. Based on the novel by Henri-Pierre Roche. *Photography:* Nestor Almendros. *Producer:* Claude Miller. *Executive Producer:* Marcel Berbert. *Production:* Les Films du Carrosse. 108 minutes.

Players: Jean-Pierre Leaud (Claude), Kika Markam (Anne), Stacey Tendeter (Muriel), Sylvia Marriott, Marie Mansart, Philippe Leotard, Irene Tunc, Mark Peterson, David Markham, Georges Delerue, Marcel Berbert, Annie Miller, Christine Pelle, Jeanne Lobre, Anne Levaslot, Sophie Jeanne, Rene Gaillard, Sophi Baker. Narrated by François Truffaut.

SUCH A GORGEOUS KID LIKE ME; 1973. *Screenplay:* Jean-Loup Dabadie, François Truffaut. Based on the novel by Henry Farrell. *Photography:* Pierre William Glenn. *Art Director:* Jean-Pierre Kohut. *Music:* Georges Delerue. *Production:* Les Films du Carrosse.

Players: Bernadette Lafont (Camille Bliss), Claude Brasseur (Murene), Charles Denner (Arthur), Guy Marchand (Sam Golden), Andre Dussollier (Stanislas Previne), Philippe Leotard (Clovis Bliss), Anne Kreis (Helene), Gilberte Geniat (Isobel Bliss), Daniele Girard (Florence Golden), Martine Ferriere (Prison Secretary), Michel Delahaye (Marchal), Annick Fougerie (School Teacher), Gaston Ouvrard (Old Prison Guard), Jacob Weizbluth (Alphonse). U.S. distribution by Columbia Pictures.

Bibliography

Books

Armes, Roy. *French Cinema Since 1946, Volume II: The Personal Style.* A. S. Barnes and Company, New Jersey, second edition, 1970.

Bazin, Andre. *What Is Cinema?* Essays selected and translated by Hugh Gray. University of California Press, Berkeley and Los Angeles, 1967.

Graham, Peter. *The New Wave.* Doubleday and Company, New York, 1968.

Kael, Pauline. *I Lost It at the Movies.* Little, Brown and Company, Boston, 1965.

Lindgren, Ernest. *The Art of the Film.* Collier Books, New York, revised edition, 1970; originally published in London, 1963.

Petrie, Graham. *The Cinema of François Truffaut.* The International Film Guide Series, A. S. Barnes and Company, New York, 1970.

Sarris, Andrew, ed. *Interviews with Film Directors.* Bobbs-Merrill Company, New York, 1967.

———. *The American Cinema.* E. P. Dutton and Company, New York, 1968.

———. *Confessions of a Cultist: On the Cinema, 1955-1969.* Simon and Schuster, New York, 1970.

Simon, John. *Movies Into Film.* New York, Dial Press.

Taylor, John Russell. *Cinema Eye, Cinema Ear.* Hill and Wang, New York, 1964.

Truffaut, François. *Hitchcock: A Definitive Study of Alfred Hitchcock.* Simon and Schuster, New York, 1967.

———. *Jules and Jim.* Translated from the French by Nicholas Fry. Simon and Schuster, New York, 1968.

Truffaut, François and Marcel Moussy. *The 400 Blows.* Edited by David Denby. Grove Press, New York, 1969.

Magazine Articles

Greenspun, Roger. A Review of STOLEN KISSES, from *On Film*, I, 1, p. 11.

Klein, Michael. "The Literary Sophistication of François Truffaut," *Film Comment* (Summer 1965), p. 24.

Sarris, Andrew. "Notes on the Auteur Theory in 1970," *Film Comment*, VI, 3 (Fall 1970), p. 7.

Shatnoff, Judith. "François Truffaut—The Anarchist Imagination," *Film Quarterly* (Spring 1963), p. 3.

Truffaut, François. "Journal of Fahrenheit 451: Parts One, Two, Three," *Cahiers du Cinema*, English edition, Nos. 5, 6, 7 (1966).

Wood, Robin. "Chabrol and Truffaut," *Movie*, No. 17 (Winter 1969-70), p. 16.

FELLINI'S FILM JOURNEY
An Essay in Seeing

Roger Ortmayer

For Fellini Film Is Film

Near the close of *The Chorus*, Fellini's quasi-documentary produced for Italian television, the director is sitting and watching the riotous clown funeral, awash in its low-clown rituals. A journalist insists on asking the logical, if inept, question, "What do you mean to say in this new production?" Fellini tries to straighten out his wits and begins to answer. A bucket abruptly falls over his head.

The meaning of what the director does lies in what he does, not in what he says. That is, a filmmaker's meaning is in images, visual and aural. The journalist wanted words to quote: he should have been watching the show instead of asking for definitions.

Fellini's emergence in the last twenty years as an artist to whom attention must be paid coincides with a fundamental cultural shift. This change is much deeper than a shuffling of forms and styles. It is rather a change of ethos, a fundamental alteration in the character of culture. A biological analogy could be used: what has happened is a mutation. The body continues many familiar characteristics from its past, but in some fundamental ways has been transformed into something unlike

A film is made, not told about.
—Fellini (Interview with Pierre Kast, in Andrew Sarris, *Interview with Film Directors*, p. 177)

Its [a film's] impetuous course modifies any preestablished scheme. Its face appears only gradually, as it is made. Basically, the paradox is that Fellini, the maker, can speak of nothing else and that, however, since he makes it, he is able to tell nothing about it.
—Kast (p. 177)

Horizon? There was no longer a horizon. I was in the wings of

67

a theater cluttered up with bits of scenery. Vertical, oblique, horizontal, all of plane geometry was awhirl. A hundred transversal valleys were muddled in a jumble of perspectives
—Antoine de Saint Exupéry (Gyorgy Kepes, *The Nature and Art of Motion;* New York: Braziller, 1965, p. [20])

anything in its history. Many aspects of this cultural mutation could be discussed, but I want to consider two that are especially pertinent to film art, namely *motion* and *communication.*

The shift from stasis to motion

A fundamental assumption which has shaped Western culture is that the normal state of being is stasis or rest. While a few Greeks may have protested that change is central, the prevailing assumption was that permanence was basic. One started with immobility. Movement was a phenomenon that altered the basic condition.

All of the arts, even music, accepted the dictum. A painting recorded a moment of a season. When the artist decided that it was finished, it was framed, a completed object. The artist was always in search of materials which would last, would assure at least a degree of permanence to his work. He experimented with pigments that resisted change, with grounds that would hold to canvas or wood in hot or cold weather, in humid or dry seasons. With frescoes he built his work into the building to last as long as the structure stood.

A sensation of 'form' . . . is an extreme rarity in life; what normally stimulates the eye is a continuous transformation in time.
—James J. Gibson (Kepes, p. 61)

Permanence was an assumed quality in architecture. Stone was of course better than wood because of stone's lastingness. Granite or marble was preferred to sandstone; they did not flake away. If stone was hard to come by, bake bricks to a stone-like quality which the original clay did not possess.

The artist also used stone when he sought to produce a "monument." Like paintings, his work was frozen. The sculptor could suggest action, but no matter how furious, it was always arrested, even the Hellenistic *Laocoon* or a victorious general on his rampant horse. The composer began and ended his music according to harmonic laws. His creation was recorded in notation and line so that it would last and could be played again and again just as the master had decided it should go. The dramatist began and resolved his play. The poet followed the rules of meter, line, and stanza.

The twentieth century has, however, so altered the world of stasis that there is no return.

The assumption that rest is normal and motion an alteration of the basic condition has been discarded along with such notions as the immutability of matter and the fixed position of the stars. It is all quite relative to where one stands and to the character of one's sensory apparatus.

The fixity of a piece of wood or chunk of stone is really an illusion. Wood and stone may seem unchanging to our touch or sight, but break them down to their fundamental character and you'll find them flowing with energy pulses and charges rather than being structured by building blocks. Energy is a flow, not a solid, impermeable mass.

"Ladies and gentlemen, it is painful but necessary to admit that we live in an age ruled by the senses and by matter. . . . An era in which—" an exceptionally loud crash of thunder drowns out the recording!
—*Temptations of Doctor Antonio*

Understanding communication

The artist, as artist, is a communicator. His art may, or may not, tell something. More importantly, he establishes relationships through his art.

In a time of messages and truths held without regard for context, the communicator

I may use abstract forms poetically, as human beings—and can use human beings as abstractly as a rectangle. O but whatever way, a

story will develop. The medium of film turns everything into story because it MOVES.
—Hans Richter, "My Experience with Movement in Painting and in Film" (Kepes, p. 156)

passed them along from himself to the recipient. The artist's truth was located in the object he created, which could symbolize a truth or give a realistic picture of it. In any case, he passed on in some reasonably rational fashion his message to the world.

But if communication is seen as establishing a relationship, if it is reciprocal rather than one-way, then the artist pulls the others into his work. The purpose is not passing truths along. It is rather establishing a process of discovery and illumination.

Just as the notion of permanence and motionless stability as the basic pattern for our natural world has collapsed, so has the conviction that underlying all else are "truths" which have an unalterable and everlasting character. We find that ideas, philosophies, and theologies are contextual and "in process." They are becoming even as they are discarded.

In such a context it is difficult to hold notions of "eternal verities" and "absolute categories." Expressed theologically, for instance, it means that knowing God is not making dogmatic claims about his omnipotence but being in relation to him, experiencing his love. One knows God in experience, not in assertion. Christians say that Jesus Christ is what God is all about—that is, the Incarnation is the reality, and that means a living, human historical experience.

What is important now is to recover our senses. We must learn to *see* more, to *hear* more, to *feel* more. Our task is not to find the maximum amount of

Communication, therefore, is participative, relational experience. Communication passes along message, but more importantly it excites and stimulates man's whole sensational apparatus. Communication is "being in communion," that is, conversing with another's whole intellectual, emotional, mental, and sensory being.

Parallel to the change we have been forced to deal with in the world of stones and wood, then, is the switch in communication. No longer can it be considered a linear progression by means of which content is passed along from the one possessing it to the expectant recipient. While such a transference of content continues as part of communication, it is only partial to the open-ended possibilities of communication in this age when, for the first time in human history, our sensory equipment is capable of almost infinite expansion. The same basic research which forced us out of the venerable building-block concept of our universe also brought in the electronic technology which extends our senses of sight and sound. We do not have to be in Philharmonic Hall to hear and see the Philharmonic Orchestra. We do not have to be at the circus to experience the combustible antics of the clowns. Radio and television provide an extension of space, and tape, videotape, and film an extension of time, that is new to human experience.

content in a work of art, much less to squeeze more content out of the work than is already there. Our task is to cut back content so that we can see the thing at all.
—Susan Sontag in *Against Interpretation* (New York: Dell, 1967), p. 14

Ours is a brand-new world of allatoneness. "Time" has ceased, "space" has vanished. We now live in a global village . . . a simultaneous happening. We are back in acoustical space. We have begun again to structure the primordial feeling. . . .
—Marshall McLuhan in *The Medium Is the Massage* (New York: Random House, 1967), p. 63

Fellini and the art of film

In another age Fellini would have been a Botticelli or a Bosch rather than a Leonardo. His vision is comic and surreal rather than realist. He served his apprenticeship, however, in a manner parallel to that of a quatrocento painter or sculptor. In early adolescence he abandoned his bourgeois home for an itinerant circus life. As a young man in his early twenties he helped with filmscripts for now

. . . the real world around him, from which he selects what he wants, yields finally a world of his own in which nothing is merely what it seems—to that extent he is still a realist—but it is also something more—

and in consequence Fellini is also something more, a 'surrealist,' as he himself puts it, in the same sense that Giotto, Botticelli, Bosch, Breughel, and Uccello were surrealists.
—John Russell Taylor *(Cinema Eye, Cinema Ear,* p. 18)

forgotten comedies. When the war ended he became involved with Roberto Rossellini in that irruption of great Italian filmmaking, working in different capacities on *Roma, Citta Aperta* and *Paisa.*

While continuing work on various of the routine jobs that filmmaking requires, he collaborated in 1948 with Rossellini on the longest section of *Amore.* That film stirred violent arguments in the Catholic church. The Cardinal of New York insisted that its story of a peasant woman taking in a tramp she felt was St. Joseph and later giving birth to a child ("my holy son") high up on a mountainside where she had been driven by the derision of the villagers was blasphemous. The film was prescient of what Fellini was to explore when he was able to take charge of filming as director.

The Rossellini films, called neo-realism, were essentially objective in style. That is, the camera was a recorder of life and places "out there." As far as possible, the landscapes were filmed on location, so that there would be no studio manipulation of the scenery. Dialogue, clothing, situations should be real, not contrived. This, of course, was based on the assumption that the real is what meets eye and ear as one walks down the street or sits in the marketplace.

During the weekend Bergman showed them [Elliott Gould and Jenny Bogart, on a rare invitation to Bergman's Faro] *The White Sheik,* one of the earliest films of his favorite moviemaker, Fellini. It was part of Berg-

The first film of which Fellini was director, *Variety Lights (Luci del Varieta),* indicated the manner in which he would amend neorealist films. Its players are a tawdry, third-rate troupe, out of step, improvising, living it up in a castle from which they are dumped to the chill of a cold morning—wanderers, dreamers, scroungers, they endure with their faded hopes and passions, rituals, rousements, and humiliations. They are more subtle and ambiguous than looking at them and hearing their talk would suggest. There are other rooms to act in and other passions to phrase than those the camera catches objectively.

We cannot say that Fellini is not objective, because he is, although his films often show a kind of world that would appear nowhere but in works by Fellini. Actually, the terms "subjective" and "objective" are as meaningless as those terms we formerly used to describe the closed, building-block world. They simply have little significance in discussing his work.

Fellini is a thoroughly filmic artist. He is often put down as being a romantic. But, as with objective and subjective, the description is irrelevant. Categories such as classical and romantic make sense in describing the eighteenth and early nineteenth centuries—they cannot be applied in today's milieu. When a critic tries, he mainly indicates his irrelevance to judge.

A romantic artist was an aberration in a period when the stable orders of classicism were accepted as the norm. Romantics were considered irrational, and that was bad because rationality was following certain logical, intellectual principles considered of the highest order. Romantics displayed strong emotion, and that was frightening, for it led toward bestiality, dominance by unruly appetites and passions. Romantics wallowed in *Sturm und Drang*, a scandalous, self-indulgent alternative to the unruffled, detached calm of the intellectual life.

Fellini's inability to stick to a predetermined course, his constant improvisation, his

man's very large private collection of films, including his own, which he reruns to study and learn from.
—Richard Merryman (*Life*, Oct. 15, 1971)

. . . for Fellini what matters first is not the outward reality but the inner reality; landscapes for him become an objective correlative to the mental and spiritual states of his characters, to be created (if with real locations then by precise choice of viewpoint, weather, time of day and so on to produce exactly the effect required)—he has, in fact, remarked on at least one occasion that what draws him most to cinema is its quality as a domain in which he can play God, in which everything is, not as it is, but as he thinks it ought to be.
—John Russell Taylor (p. 18)

For me, working on a film is a journey—I've said this so often that I hardly believe it any more.

You don't take a journey in the abstract, but consider the exigencies that come up from hour to hour, your own mood, things that are impossible to predict. All that's required is an availability; you must allow yourself to be transported. Or, more precisely, you must put yourself in the hands of the thing that is to be born.
—Fellini (Interview with Tullio Kerich, in Kerich, ed., *Juliet of the Spirits*, p. 41)

Oh, in those two-reelers, they didn't bother to give you any character or name or anything, things just started happening.
—Buster Keaton (Interview with Christopher Bishop)

The cinema in fact has a strong resemblance to circus.
—Fellini (Interview with Fellini on Belgian television, printed in Suzanne Budgen's *Fellini*)

delight in coincidence is no more irrational than their opposites. It is irrational only if rationality is equated with the rules of logic the rationalists invented. Fellini's mind is one of the most alert and perceptive of the twentieth century—that he will often start a film or a scene with a sketch rather than with words is simply his way of conceptualizing and planning his work. He thinks visually. Does that make him irrational? Only if rationality is limited to the vocabulary of those who insist that meaning must be put into words, surely one of the most irrational claims ever to bedevil the human scene.

The cinema era is still in the process of creating pertinent criticism. When the picture moves *actually* instead of by implication, when motion is the normal rather than rest, when the technology is integral to the art, when the fixed points of reference are no longer fixed but themselves in process, then new strategies of evaluation must be devised.

This is why Fellini is so often misunderstood. Understanding Fellini is being immersed in viewing and hearing his films. One understands only in the seeing—which in a way makes an essentially verbal discussion such as this quite irrelevant. This bit of labor can be justified only if it stimulates the reader to go back to seeing Fellini. It is made up of a few notes to help the conversation along. Perhaps it will also help clear away some of the rubbish that has accumulated as film criticism—which evaluates film as if it were literature, or stage drama, or sociology, or psychology, or—heaven help us—theology.

2

Fellini, Artist

One of the most prejudicial notions from the old systems of categories is the notion of "fine arts." The fine arts were the arts that had no utilitarian role, were distinct from crafts. They presumably were made for delight in creation and the status they gave the possessor. They were about the significant, the beautiful, and the exemplary. Because they were also useless, they added up to superior.

Motion pictures were at first excluded from the rarified atmosphere of the arts. Nickelodeon and then the longer, more coherent films were beneath even contemptuous notice. This had nothing to do with their general popularity. In fact, the more the general public delighted in cinema, the more contemptuous the regard of those identified with the fine arts.

Finally, shortly before World War II, a few students of culture began to use the term "art" when discussing motion pictures, though most often it was qualified by the label "popular." Such a distinction persists today, a cultural lag. It should, however, no longer be necessary to argue the cause of film as art—certainly not after Fellini and the out-

The new art is sympathetic because in an age of total disruption it has conserved the will-to-image; because it is inclined to force the image, even though the means and parts be antagonistic.
—Hugo Ball *(Dada Fragments*, Mar. 30, 1917, p. 53)

The cows in India, not understanding traffic lights, cross intersections whenever they reach them.
—John Cage

. . . photography is clearly the most important event in the history of plastic arts. Simultaneously a liberation and an accomplishment, it has freed Western painting, once and for all, from its ob-

75

session with realism and allowed it to recover its aesthetic autonomy.
—Andre Bazin in *What Is Cinema?* (Berkeley: University of California, 1967), p. 16

Gelsomina, dressed as a clown, is singing a little song and accompanying herself with comic and pathetic miming. Zampano, stripped to the waist as for his performance, accompanies her on the harmonica. The show is taking place in the open space in front of a big farm, which has high walls, black and massive, like those of an ancient fortress. In the yard a wedding breakfast is spread. . . .
—Original script for *La Strada* by Fellini and Pinelli (Budgen, p. 105)

It *[La Strada]* is a film of insights, of things felt rather than thought, but felt in the context of our moral situation, which we know but cannot ra-

burst of creative film activity around the globe after World War II. Many artists who might once have been painters, sculptors, dramatists, or novelists were drawn toward films.

It is impossible for me to forget my first encounter with *La Strada* when by chance I went into a New York "art theater." I was not prepared, having paid my way in with some kind of vague expectation of another Italian neo-realist production. What I met was a great work of art, and I knew it much more surely than if some critic had given it such a stamp. In fact, had I read the critics, I probably would not have made it to the film, since most of them put *La Strada* down. They too expected neo-realism, and what they got was a journey into awareness that they apparently were unable to take. Neo-realism as film had developed an ideology, a set of cultic rules, and when judged by those rules, Fellini's film did not do well. That the standards had nothing almost to do with what Fellini accomplished did not stop the critics' harsh evaluations. It was similar to the way earlier critics had judged Stravinsky's *Rite of Spring*. When they appeared at the Paris Opera, they expected something like Verdi or Gounod; they got Stravinsky. Therefore, Stravinsky was the target of rotten fruit and verbal scorn. He did not fit.

La Strada is a mysterious film, mysterious in the religious sense. In viewing the film one is in "seeingfeelhearing." One knows, but has difficulty making the knowing rationalization. Taken in isolation, incidents and scenes may be outrageously sentimental, incongruous, even contrived. The artist makes them right and proper.

La Strada is love and indifference and gentleness and violence. It is not about persons who are violent or gentle, but is about the incarnation, the real appearance, of the destroyer (Zampano, played by Anthony Quinn) and of holy innocence (Gelsomina, played by Giulietta Masina).

Gelsomina is naive. Naiveté is one of the most tricky characteristics to reveal, which may be one of the reasons why most Renaissance painters wanted to do the Annunciation. To make both angel and virgin believable, in her innocence as contrasted with his knowingness, calls for consummate skills of craft and interpretation. To do naiveté in a full-length film, with Gelsomina almost always present, requires artistic genius. Both farce and mawkishness edge themselves in. Farce often trades on the naive, making the credulous person a laughingstock. And when the unsophisticated person is a child of nature, she turns into a simpleton, embarrassing us with her presence.

Gelsomina is completely credulous. She wants to believe and does believe even when Zampano slaps her around, abandons her, makes her feel ridiculous. But when he pays a little attention, introduces her as his wife, makes her feel a part of his act, she responds with joy, holding nothing back.

Gelsomina is at one with nature. She is as water, which in *La Strada* has a sacramental presence. She is a holy one, being born from the waters and returning to them in death. She hears secretive sounds. She is deeply

tionalize. "The good that I would I do not, but the evil which I would not, that I do."
—Budgen (p. 20)

I prefer a dimension whose contours are lost in obscurity but which is more vast, to a little, well-lighted construction that is a prisoner of very rigid walls. It aware of fire. She is close to the soil, planting tomatoes, though she will not be around to harvest them.

Such ingenuousness, spontaneity, affinity with nature is a delicately subtle communion and difficult to communicate. But whenever it seems that we are going to be pushed into the kind of difficult emotional feeling we have when in the presence of the mentally handicapped, we find that instead of being embarrassed we can relate to the complete guilelessness of Gelsomina. She is not only authentically a whole person, she is more alive, more really a person, than we can ever be without holding under cover our inner selves. Gelsomina has an indwelling life that is open to all of life, trying to communicate worth, to go beneath the surfaces of both persons and nature.

Zampano, a circus strongman, takes Gelsomina with him in the first place because of the death of her sister Rosa. He simply replaces one woman with the other. Although Rosa's death takes place before the beginning of this film, we feel that in some manner Zampano's violence and cruelty have caused her death. Women simply cannot bear up to him; but he needs them.

Zampano's cruelty is not deliberate. He is hardly enough of a thinker to deliberate anything. Nor is he a sadist. But he does destroy, a mindless smashing of everything and everybody around him. His loving is as brutal as his circus act, in which he wraps a chain around his chest and breaks the links as he expands the rib cage.

His murder of Il Matto, the tightrope aerialist, is an act of violence wildly incommensurate with the provocation. Il Matto is as free

of gravity as Zampano is bound by it. He is an
elf, Zampano a grizzly bear. Il Matto helps
Gelsomina know herself as a human being,
and she finds her humanity in relation to
Zampano, whom she can now both defy and
love. But Zampano cannot understand. Il
Matto is what he is not; so, resentful and
frustrated, he smashes Il Matto, pitches him
into a creek, and throws his car down after
him. With that Gelsomina breaks. She will do
some more chores, survive for a while, but her
identity, her being is shattered. She is finished, a frail pilgrim who goes on down the
road, but without awareness; and it was
awareness that made her so precious.

When Michelangelo, in his last year,
sculpted such poignant works as the
Rondanini *Pieta*, his contemporaries dismissed
them as unfinished, distorted, rough, and un-
couth. They preferred the high craftsmanship
of the Vatican Pieta, done a half century
earlier with the exuberant skill of the young
Michelangelo. Their taste for the classic realism of the young artist and his attention to
naturalistic detail fitted the notion of the
artist as one who makes beautiful and exemplary objects. The mature Michelangelo, however, was no longer interested in such criteria.
Rather, he was concerned to emphasize suffering. Death, with its involvement for the survivors, deprived the bodies of athletic beauty.
Instead they are roughhewn, angular silhou-
ettes.

Draftsmanship is *about* a record, a more or
less skillful representation. It is refined by
skill in using the rules. Which was what was
expected of the painter up to the time of
Leonardo and Michelangelo. Painting was not

"You killed him.
It's nice out here.
He told me to stay
with you. We need
more wood. The fire
is going out."
—Gelsomina in *La
Strada*

O human folly! O
living madness! Sim-
ple people shall car-

ry many lights to il-
luminate the route
of those who have
lost their sight.
—Leonardo

. . . Painting and
sculpture can no
longer soothe the
soul turned towards
that Love divine
which, to possess us,
opens wide its arms.
—Michelangelo

one of the "seven arts," but a craft much like making barrels or jewelry.

Many of the Renaissance artists, however, sought to go in a different direction, one which they identified as art. It was something other than *about* what was pictured—instead, a probing of its being. They wanted other than a portrait record. They sought an interpretation of the inside life of the one pictured. As artists, their work had to *be*, not just be *about*.

Fellini's films *are*, in this sense. What they are about is certainly not irrelevant, but the story content is hardly their treasure. What adds up to art is relationship: of people, of images, of environments. These are given in an unequivocally visual form, especially the films beginning with *La Dolce Vita*.

To say that Fellini deals with the miseries of the sweet life, with the discrepancies between reality and illusion, between the urban life and personal freedom, etc. is not much help. What he does do, superbly, is to show, to reveal, to illuminate life. Sometimes he does it with characters who have verism. More often he does it with characters who do not. Some, in fact, are outrageously improbable.

Like Michelangelo, it seems that the older Fellini gets, the more distraught and ambiguous his situations become. The difference between the Sistine Chapel ceiling and *The Last Judgment* is something like the jump from *The White Sheik* to *Fellini Satyricon*. The *Satyricon* is not easy to take; neither is *The Last Judgment*. The obvious gives way to the complex, the laugh to the shudder.

Like the popes of the Council of Trent

era, who found *The Last Judgment* too car-
nal and too disturbing, many critics have
assigned Fellini to oblivion for being both
too sensual and too esoteric. In the lexicon
of such critics, he has become self-
indulgent. Presumably that means that he
has followed his own vision rather than the
preferences of the critics. In fact, however,
all great artists have insisted on their vision.
Michelangelo's squabbles with his patron,
the pope, were also considered self-
indulgent.

Juliet of the Spirits deals with a stranded
marriage and a woman who must find a
secure foundation for her life. The distortions of a relationship that has slipped
away, false attachments and teachings,
treacherous myths, mixed-up feelings, superficial expectations are all themes. They are
dealt with, however, through descriptive
images rather than through narrative.

Certainly Fellini tapped an emotionally
charged and up-to-date area of existence for
modern man and woman. He could have
taken the obvious route of the sexual
triangle—disintegration into bitchiness or
forlornness, quarrels generating quarrels, all of
them fed with suspicion. As it happens,
all of these are involved, but loaded with
such nuances and subtleties that they become sideshows, even trivia in the clusters
of revelation.

Juliet's house, prim, proper, and luxuri-
ous with its manicured garden, makes us
recall, as the film begins, a Magritte painting of a house through which clouds float
serenely or in which the doors are cutouts
of invisible inhabitants. It is Juliet's own

. . . The Clowns, a
lamentable piece of
self-indulgence,
self-congratulation,
and self-parody dis-
guised as a docu-
mentary, was not
given the swift kick
in its clownish rear
it deserved. . . .
—John Simon
*(Intellectual Di-
gest,* Sept. 1971,
p. 10)

This "meeting" with
the public is a gift,
an almost clownlike
calling, *a la* Barnum
or Buffalo Bill. The
factor of communi-
cating is uncon-
scious. I've never
considered for a
moment whether
the public will un-
derstand or not. The
public is an abstract
entity; one cannot
foresee what it will
do. The captivating
quality [some might
call it pandering]
that you find in my
pictures, if it is
there, is completely
instinctive.
—Fellini (Kerich,
p. 51)

To demand from
others a fidelity to
ourselves is mon-
strous; it is an anti-
religious thought.
The only true fidel-

ity is to oneself and to one's own destiny, absolutely respecting one's individuality.
—Fellini (Kerich, p. 63)

image of propriety. Nothing is out of place. Furnishings are all in good taste, conventionally modern.

Yet the house is possessed by spirits. One of the maids is primly watchful, and we later see that her face is also that of an eerie saint. The other maid is titillating and curious and suggests exciting, if off-bounds, behavior.

It is the wedding anniversary of Juliet and her husband, Giorgio. She has the dinner table set with candles. Giorgio wants to know if the electricity is off—he has forgotten the date. The intimacy she had hoped for is made impossible by the invasion of a noisy, prying, swirling party of friends. The celebration turns out to be the wrong kind.

Both Juliet and Giorgio are victimized by their false, unsustainable attachments and expectations, although the focus is on the woman. Fellini does not moralize. He is too strong as an artist to give us a documentary on marriage; he provides us with illuminations. And they come through the eye, not by being told to us in words.

The masculination of the woman is one of the most horrible things possible.
—Fellini (Kerich, p. 62)

Like Gelsomina in *La Strada*, Juliet is a natural person, surrounded by extravagant situations, persons, and events. She tries on a variety of wigs, then discards them in favor of her own hairdo. She unconsciously pushes up her cheek bones with her fingers—she is getting older and her skin is beginning to sag a bit.

Juliet continues to stare at her husband, but without

Giorgio is guilt-filled, knowing he has been false to his wife. But where does the real falseness lie? In his relations with an-

other woman? Or in his expectations of a
marriage which are themselves false? Can a
marriage "succeed" if the precognitions are
illusory? And are cognitions themselves
destructive? Is marriage more a matter of
living than of definitions? What mean the
ties of marriage (recalling that this is pre-
Vatican II Italy, where marriage bonds are
legally and religiously indissoluble)?
The focus, however, is on the woman.
And she has to come to her own reality,
really be her natural self, rather than a
woman distorted by living according to
false expectations. Is the issue really Giorgio's mistress? Or is it her own being? The
harmony and structured order of life about
her keep dissolving into fantastic illusory environments. Counsels of beauty are given by a
disgusting, vomiting old man, and the chaste
and the pure saints and nuns act out
charades of purity with false angel wings
and roast little girls on iron grids over
flaming coals.
Other possibilities are offered by Susy's
gloriously erotic house, which seems somehow
or other to have connections with Juliet's own
place, although never visible in the long shots
of house and garden. It is a place of sensuous
contours and marvellous color. No cognitive
contemplation at Susy's, but plenty of
voluptuous relaxation. The stairway up is a
curved invitation to sexual pleasure, the
Venus-shell entry to a tubal slide down to a
pleasure wallow bath.
Yet at Susy's house Juliet is always outside
or unaccommodated. She's too natural for its
stimulations, which are as artificial as the
ghastly Bhishma's admonition: "Why don't

looking at him, as if
his place were emp-
ty.
GIORGIO
(surprised): What
are you doing?
JULIET: Nothing.
Just getting used to
looking as if you
weren't there.
GIORGIO (discon-
certed and cautious)
I don't understand.
    —Juliet of the
    Spirits

In place of a herme-
neutics we need an
erotics of art.
    —Susan Sontag
(Against Interpre-
tation, p. 14)

A beautiful woman
makes me feel more
religious.
—Grandfather in
*Juliet of the Spir-
its*

You think the
grandfather has no
precedent? Isn't he
a little like the Fool
in *La Strada?* Affec-
tionate, extravagant,
something of a jest-
er?
—Fellini (Kerich,
p. 44)

you become beautiful like me?" Such beauty is too awful to be beautiful.

Susy, however, is a liberator. She is also Grandfather's wonderful ballerina. Grandfather releases Juliet from the church's ascetic exercises and pageants, which seems to be done in the cause of an anti-clerical liberalism. But when all the forces of convention threaten to hem him in, he flies off in the rickety primitive plane, plainly liberated, with his loved Susy.

Juliet's liberation is not simple, not linear. The exorcism of dividing spirits will not come through unrestrained escape, nor anarchy. She has to free herself of false status and conventions.

Long before the Women's Liberation movement, Juliet was forced to see that her status as a woman did not come through her ties to a man. The conventional sexual, rational, or religious escapades would do nothing for her being. She had to be really free, to break out of the circle of spirits that made her not a woman, but a captive. She had to break such false ties to being—but can she be free of time? The clock keeps ticking, the cheeks sag, the heels click down a corridor like the seconds on a clock.

She cannot escape time, those clicks keep going. But she will be a free person, in possession of herself. Part of the falseness she has been trying to live with is regarding time as the enemy. Rather time *is,* and Juliet *is,* and to be is to join the procession of free creatures.

Before *Juliet of the Spirits,* except for the brief exercise of Dr. Antonio, Fellini used black and white film. The switch in *Juliet* toward using a variety of colors was an astonishing experience for those who first saw the film.

Strictly speaking, of course, Fellini had always used color. The differences between solid black and blinding white are shaded through a whole scale of value. In black and white film, shapes are readily identifiable, but when it comes to such nuances as distinguishing Burgundy wine from Chablis, it is difficult. The use of colors adds multivaried dimensions for the artist. An expressive impact is added. Emotional communication is expanded. The visual is stimulated. In black and white the line of narrative action is direct. Varied colors make a diffusion, or clustering, of the images more potent.

Color has a direct and spontaneous effect. It is vividly sensuous. It both orients and scatters energy. Seeing color has something to do with the wavelength of vibrations, and our bodies seem to react and respond to their intensities. Exactly what the relationship is, is still debatable in the area of perceptual phenomena. In any case, there is considerable evidence that in response to some color and color combinations the human organism tends to open outward. Other colors seem to cause it to withdraw, to concentrate inward.

Fellini does not use color symbolically. That is, certain colors do not stand for certain objects, situations, persons, etc. As we shall note, such is usually the case with Fellini's imagery. It is seldom symbolic in such a mechanical sense. Color is, however, apt to his imagery. In fact, color becomes imagery.

An aspect of the revolutionary character of

If drawing is of the spirit and color of the senses, you must draw first, to cultivate the spirit and to be able to lead color into spiritual paths.
—Matisse

In *Juliet* . . . color is an essential part of the film. I don't think I would have done it in black and white. It is a type of fantasy that is developed through colored illuminations. As you know, color is a part not only of the language but also of the idea and the feeling of the dream. Colors in a dream are concepts, not approximations or memories.
—Fellini (Kerich, p. 35)

A yellow circle will reveal a spreading movement outwards from the center which almost markedly approaches the spectator . . . a blue circle develops a concentric movement (like a snail hiding in its shell) and moves away from the spectator.
—Fellini (Kerich, p. 35)

The painter gives to his painting a steady, unchangeable light. Color is an extremely personal factor, even on a psychological level. My green is not your green, nor that of a third person. Whoever paints can choose precisely the shade of color he wants. Someone may think that the same thing can be done in film, that it's enough to put the light on the element you want to bring out, and your green comes out. Let's say it can be like this, although in fact there is a fluid interchange among the colors of a scene. . . . You realize that certain luminous areas are submerged in dark-

modern art has been this change in the way in which the painter uses color. Traditionally it had been used as attempted verism. Color corresponded to the objects, scapes, clothing, and faces which were represented by the painter. Or color was used allegorically and symbolically. For· example, purple indicated royalty, white stood for purity, and red stood for blood.

When, however, Matisse painted a portrait of his wife, early in this century, and her hair showed up purple, he was not saying she was of royal blood, or that she dyed her hair that color. For him, it was purely a matter of art—no symbolism, no verisimilitude. That approach was to be taken by most of the influential artists who followed in this century. It was not a red apple that appealed to the artist, but redness itself. Color was to be used as color, not color as representation.

Although the art concept of color had been common among artists for half a century before *Juliet of the Spirits*, it was by no means common among filmmakers. When color film first showed up on the commercial screen in the thirties, such a movie as *Vanity Fair* shook some of us with a kind of visual excitement we had never encountered before. But as with the early cinema, which deserted its pristine filmic sense for secondhand dramatic patterns, so color film deserted color as filmic art for color verism. Color films were common enough but they were conventional. Technicians devised complicated formula controls to transfer the color of what was filmed as accurately as possible.

The same formulas transferred to color electronic film in television. In 1967 I conceived a show for CBS-TV, proposing the use of color in painterly fashion. Making the show almost drove the technicians crazy; it certainly did force their control gauges into surprising antics. To use color as color, that is, to use it filmicly rather than as naturalistic representation, was to violate all the film formulas for color use!

When Fellini turned to color, it was predictable only that he would not do it according to formula. Nor did he.

The color in *Juliet* is sensational. By that I do not mean that Fellini sought to produce some kind of public excitement. Rather, the color is used as art, to heighten perceptivity. Seeing the film, one feels more keenly, more exquisitely, than he could otherwise. The film is a full sense apprehension. It is sensate.

The color makes one aware of Juliet's harmonies and conflicts. It makes the viewer alive to and responsive to her options. Her red dress when she goes to Susy's house involves us in the erotic possibilities open to her. Both fire and water have an aliveness not met even in such a fine movie as *La Strada*. The opening shots of Juliet's house are the colors of primness and conventionality. First seeing the materialist doctor against the background of brilliant orange chair and tent makes an aggressive complement to Juliet in white, in a white deck chair, against white sand and white sky. Such sensational use of color is one of the great moments in film art.

Fellini went on to other filmic possibilities of color in *Satyricon*. Almost all of the critics missed this achievement, nosing around as they were for narrative lines and symbolic representations. They found the story line

ness and others have taken on unforeseeable reflections.
—Fellini (Kerich, p. 36)

I must say that the use of color according to a rigorous plan is not possible.
—Fellini (Kerich, p. 36)

The dreamer can see a red meadow, a green horse, a yellow sky—and they're not absurdities. They are images tempered with the feeling that inspires them.
—Fellini (Kerich, p. 35)

The eye must be stimulated by . . . curiosity to look and discover around it the multiple aspects of reality.
—Fellini (Kast, p. 187)

confused and the symbolism confused, so they concluded that Fellini's "self-indulgence" had gotten out of bounds. Few of them seemed able to realize that they were being treated to a masterpiece of filmic art, not the other thing they were opting for.

I first saw *Satyricon* in Europe with French (or was it German?) subtitles. I do not recall, because I paid no attention to subtitles. I could follow neither the verbal nor the titled language easily, so I accommodated myself to a visual experience, a highly rewarding one, and "correct." The sound track is a jumble of dialects and music anyway.

The colors of *Satyricon* are as wondrous as Fellini's juxtapositions of faces and events. They are the colors of dream and unremitting, orgiastic imagination. Every point in *Satyricon* is invested with mixes of redness, whiteness, brownness, greenness. The faces as masks, the walls, the sea, the villas, all are color-alive.

Fellini has said that to do *Satyricon* was to do away with the Renaissance inventions of antiquity, or the nineteenth century's, or our own. They were all invented Romes, unhistorical histories. He wanted the Rome without Christ; the Rome where tickets were sold to the amphitheaters to watch people die, the Rome without any of the touches of compassion and love which are what Christ is.

Color is both an affliction and a tension. Different hues drain each other off, saturate with brightness, diminish and gain strength. There is little "pure" color, the simple energy of a single tone. The film is too complex and ambiguous for that. Rather the vibrations are mixed and complex.

... A film is perhaps a weapon against definitions.
—Fellini (Kast, p. 189)

When one shows a world that is open, baroque, delirious, demanding, clamorous, multiple, contradictory, a farce and a tragedy, there is no reason at all to suppose that it must be less accessible immediately, than a world enclosed in conventions. . . .
—Fellini (Kast, p. 190)

Photographers identify film speed, etc., and their relation to the light available in terms of "temperature." The color reactions provoke sensations of "warm" and "cold." Such "temperature readings" are apt for both *Juliet* and *Satyricon*. Withdrawal, centering, aggression, expanding, contracting—all help us to see the alienation and integration in these movies. Dominant in *Satyricon* is alienation; in *Juliet*, integration.

On the making of symbols and images

To insist that in *Satyricon* Fellini's mixture of hues is dynamic, full of tension, while the use of more primary colors strengthens the quality of wholeness in *Juliet*, is not to point to instances of color symbolism. What must not be done is to interpret the colors allegorically. This is a temptation in dealing with Fellini, since his imager, is so varied, strange, strong, and provocative. Too many commentators have fallen into the trap of allegorizing Fellini, making his images into symbols that "stand for" something else.

In art, a work is called symbolic when individual representations can be understood only by finding the keys to their underlying references. For example, a 1510 drawing by Leonardo da Vinci shows a boat with a tree for the mast, a wolf at the helm, steering by a compass with rays pointing toward a glittering eagle on a globe. It would all be quite incomprehensible if one did not know that the boat is the church, the wolf is the papacy, and the pointing toward the eagle and globe a pointing toward the emperor, or world dominion. To see the da Vinci drawing is to know the fig-

I am insistent on the dreamlike character of the film *[Satyricon]*. Everything will be disconnected, fragmentary. And at the same time mysteriously homogenous. Every detail will stand out on its own account, isolated, dilated, absurd, monstrous. . . .
—Fellini (Conversation with Alberto Moravia, in Dario Zanelli, ed., *Fellini's Satyricon*, p. 27)

ures stand for something else. They have definite factual referents.

Symbolic usage was popular in a closed world of accepted order and separations. A lily in art would always stand for the Virgin Mary, just as a tripartite aureole stood for divinity and a carpenter's level stood for inexorable justice. Meanings were separate from the things themselves. The things pointed to or stood for something else.

I do not think this is the case with Fellini and it is important to get the distinction. Fellini is too existentialist, too modern, to go in for symbolism, in spite of the vivid imagery.

In *La Strada* there is a memorable scene when Zampano has deserted Gelsomina, going off with Redhead. Gelsomina is disconsolate, sitting on a cobblestone cart. We first hear a horse's hooves on the stones, then its hindquarters appear. The horse is unattended, not even a bridle. It disappears down the street into the night. The scene has been put together with simple, if incongruous, pieces: a despairing woman, a piebald horse and a cobblestone street. To attempt an interpretation by noting what a horse stands for, or a cobblestone roadway, or night, or a girl sitting on the curb would not only be irrelevant, but silly. The scene has touches of the comic, but the overwhelming sense is of inner anguish and lostness. A woman on a curb and a wandering horse—that is the genius of Fellini.

Many of his other images are more tempting to find symbolic meanings in. Water, fire, fountains, city squares, circuses, clowns, apparitions from the sea, etc., recur in film after film, and they seem to mean much the

Any ideas I have immediately become concrete in sketches or drawings. Sometimes the very ideas are born when I'm drawing. Gelsomina, for example, came out of a drawing.
—Fellini (Kerich, p. 34)

same thing time after time. But even that
much definiteness is not the same as standing
for something else. Their meaning is innate in
what they are. The character of water is different from the character of fire. The fountain
quenches thirst, fire burns away. The city
square is made for crowds of people, and
somehow, things are not right when the
usually bustling square is deserted.

La Dolce Vita (1960) opens with a sequence that has jolted some religious sensibilities. A helicopter is carrying a huge Christ-
figure over rooftops, through the air, to the
Vatican. The rotors provide a kind of aureole
to the sentimentalized figure, bouncing along
to its destination. The figure is the kind of
pretty religiosity so often identified with religious art. The arms are outstretched, the robes
flow about the body. The work is patently
false and in bad taste. Girls sunbathing on
rooftops cheerfully wave as it goes by, which
would seem to be more attention than the
statue would merit in itself. But it is skipping
through the air—so, "Hello!"

Again, the image is what it is, not something else. A work of sentimental religiosity
tied to a work of contemporary technology—
vastly incongruous, vastly provoking. It works
as image, not symbol.

8½ (1963) begins with another of those
aerial apparitions Fellini delights in. Guido
(Marcello Mastroianni) is caught in a suffo-
cating traffic jam, desperate inside his car,
starved for breath. He escapes, floating as a
kite above the seashore, a rope tied to his leg.
A horseman comes galloping along the beach.
His command brings the free flyer down, like
Icarus. Fantasy, yes; symbolism, no. *8½* does,

however, skirt as closely to the allegorical as possible, without falling into the pit.

The title is the most direct, unambiguous part of the film. It just happens that Fellini the movie maker had finished seven and a half films as director—the *Temptation of Doctor Antonio* episode from *Boccaccio '70* being the one-half. So the new film is *8½*.

Guido is a filmmaker, and he is fed up with laboring to make a new film, suffocated with it all. He has his production responsibilities, but writers, producers, stars are all too much. He wants inspiration, even as he is tempted to synthetic work.

In the film we are flooded with scenes by association and images mothered by invention. Sorting them into any narrative continuity is difficult. Sometimes it is the film we see, sometimes what the director is thinking or dreaming about the film, sometimes his own associations and activities. Guido is divided in spirit and in life. Where is his wholeness? In his work? His ideas? His friends and loves?

He is tempted by his version of the Platonic ideal. When Claudia (Claudia Cardinale) appears, she is in white. Guido is at the fountain of the spa, where the recuperative waters are given to the tired, the jaded, the worn-out, the convalescing. Rather than being served by one of the regular attendants, he is given the cup of restoration by the woman in white.

Claudia in white, the cup filled at the fountain of regenerative water—such images do seem to call for an allegorical interpretation. They stand for something specific, that is, the detached, rarified, intellectualized purity of the classic ideal. Appropriately, Fellini uses

The characters of this film are a mixture of themselves and what Fellini would like them to be. To try to part the waters is hopeless.
—Deena Boyer
(The 200 Days of 8½, p. 157)

such standardized images when they work; for example, when it is the world of idealism that tempts Guido, then the symbols of the two-story world are utilized.

In *Juliet of the Spirits* the Venus shell and Eve and the serpent flash by, venerable images of the goddess of love and of erotic temptation. Religious images abound in most Fellini films. Such figures are there because in their presence the recognition of the scene is established. That is, when he deals with erotic love he also plays with Venus images. Such usage, however, should not be transferred to the multitude of Fellini images. For example, some Freudian commentators have had their usual field day with Fellini. In their view every image has something to do with sex. There is no possibility of anything's being upright, limp, or prostrate, there can be no doors, entrances, or exits, but that they have their male or female genital associations. Going in or going out is always part of a sexual act. If a room is curved it is feminine, if rectilinear it is male. Such nonsense is worse than a dry well, it is mischievous. It spawns the Freudian's preconceived notions, hardly dealing with Fellini's lively images.

This is the main trouble with symbolic theory. Symbols have meaning because of the preconceptions to which they are attached. They hold up in worlds where status and order are defined. Where caste and class are binding, there the sign language defining the boundaries makes sense.

This, however, is not Fellini's world. He demands an involvement in life, not an abstraction from it. It is somewhat ironic that Freudians are among the worst of contemporary abstractionists. Convinced as they are that sex is the key to meaning, one would think that they would take their own commitment seriously. Instead, and sadly, they prefer to symbolize it. Symbolization is often a convenient way of avoiding coming to terms with a work of art.

Fellini is deeply immersed in man-woman (and sometimes neuter) relationships. His series of films utilizing his wife, Giulietta Masina (*The White Sheik, La Strada, Il Bidone, Nights of Cabiria, Juliet of the Spirits*), explore with delicacy, and yet profoundly, what it is to be a free, whole person. When Masina does not dominate, it is liable to be Anita Ekberg (*La Dolce Vita, Temptation of Doctor Antonio*). In the end, Fellini usually comes down with the free person, whose freedom comes in life involvement, not in escape or in abstractions about it. Thus the overlapping, involved, often ambiguous images and scenes of *8½* penetrate into life, with its improvisations and incongruities, its passions and doubts, its plans and frustrations. It opts into life, not out of it.

It is necessary to see *8½* (as well as *La Dolce Vita, Juliet, Satyricon*) several times to get real enjoyment from it. The overlaps and focus are varied and shift in clusters rather than line continuities. We are used to the continuities of narrative film, which makes it difficult to deal with the different rhythm of *8½*. It is something like music which changes beat in the middle of the piece, abandons key signatures, and then adopts them again.

The problem of the Ideal is that it seems so pure and so true. There is a feeling of oughtness about it, especially when we feel weary

. . . As for Federico, not for an instant will he quit his camera and his actors. His face is drawn, and he needs a shave. From time to time someone will bring him some cheese, some "extraordinary sausages," a glass of whiskey. He smiles, and thanks them, eats, drinks, makes a wry joke, laughs—and locks himself up again in his inner vision.
—Boyer (p. 67)

and frustrated with our lives. So Guido longs for Claudia—she is really tempting. But when he reaches, she is always just out of grasp. She is beautiful, always temptingly beautiful, but without passion. Wife (Luisa) and mistress (Carla) are also enmeshed in Guido's life. Luisa is elegant, Carla vulgar. Luisa's role is horribly complex. She is wife, and as wife she must fit, and endure, many roles. Carla has only to be there when Guido wants her.

But the patterns are really complicated when we finally realize that sometimes it is a screen test we are seeing, not the real (or is it the real) life? Is it Carla or another woman in Carla's clothes? Or the pseudo-Luisa? Private or film life? Or is the private life the way into the film experience?

Sitting in a theater seat watching 8½, we are bewildered, even shocked, when we realize that what seemed to be the screen tests are the film. Then too, there is Guido's vivid memory. In the harem scene he relives the mother-coddled days of childhood, the comfort of being spoiled by women, the sense of being the male master and cracking his whip. The whole thing is anything but erotic, but for Guido it is gratifying to get away from the intellectual writers, producers, actors, journalists, and other colleagues who harry, criticize, cajole, and otherwise make his life miserable.

Other childhood events are hardly so comforting. The scene of the sexless priest court trying the boy after the seashore visit to the bloated prostitute Saraghina is a hideous moment. Can he ever take any confidence in a church whose image is that of humorless, sealed up prosecutor?

Not that Guido cannot himself act the part

Are you another one of those who

like films in which nothing happens? —Guido in *8½*

. . . We are stifled by words, images, sounds—none of which has any reason to exist! One must educate oneself to silence. . . . Guido, my friend— silence, emptiness, nothingness are so beautiful, so pure! If one cannot have everything, then the only real perfection is nothingness. —Daumier in *8½*

And now Guido knows Daumier is wrong, and that he will make his film. He sees himself in the center of the arena under the towers, with his megaphone, directing the parade of clowns, led by little Guido in white. A great white curtain hides the stairway. . . . —Boyer (p. 207)

of judge. The carping intellectualizing of Daumier (who is given a French name and made a Frenchman only after the filming is done and Fellini is at work on dubbing sound and dialogue) finally becomes too much. A little gesture and Daumier is condemned to oblivion (execution?) and Guido is free to create, to go on and finish the film. Daumier is the utter rationalist. He cannot see an image, delight in sound, encounter an environment without referring it to a rational judgment. What does it mean? Why is it there? Make it make sense!

But Guido's (that is, Fellini's) way is to do a lot of heavy planning, to work and struggle with a set, to argue and cajole the actors, and then to decide it all by using a wandering chicken for the same scene. But should he have stuck with the script? Is he being irresponsible to spend so much money, time, and effort and decide the whole thing by happenstance?

Realities, memories, symbols, and images are subjected to a rigorous censorship by Fellini. The cutting room gets many of the most fascinating scenes. Or weren't they ever really shot? At the big publicity party given by the producer to force Guido's hand, he is so badgered by the importuning company that he crawls beneath the heavy food table and commits suicide by shooting himself. From then on the problems resolve themselves merrily, and the film ends up with a circus clown band led by the child Guido.

I ask so many questions in reflecting on *8½* and its images because Fellini leaves much of the story to the participant-viewer. It has taken films, and Fellini, a long time to get to where they realize that the spectator might also participate in the creative act. The creative image in *8½*, Guido's scenario and working film, can be, perhaps ought to be, filled in by the viewer. Conventional symbolism leaves little room for such a relationship. It is too defined to be preconceived. We already know the symbol's meaning.

Fellini always surprises us. Images jostle each other and us, and we realize that in dealing with them different possibilities and levels are possible. Some will be discarded. Some are exciting entries. But in any case we are asked to go along the journey, and our joining the pilgrims makes of the journey something else than it could otherwise have been.

The scenario is out the window. This is sheer delirium. Every day Fellini goes a little further beyond the limit we ordinary people had put to his impetuosity. From the balcony Giulietta Masina and Fellini's sister watch the strange battle that is today's ration of madness.
—Boyer (p. 163)

On the filmmaker playing God

In a conversation with Roberto Rossellini in October of 1971, I recalled an observation of his about neo-realistic film as an "act of humility towards life." I twisted that by wondering what was meant by his being humble toward a camera. He did not blink, but told me how strongly he felt that his job as filmmaker was simply to give the camera a chance to see and record. The camera does the seeing. With it he had to be honest and humble.

When in an interview on Belgian television in 1962 Fellini was asked what he thought of the definition of neo-realism as an act of humility towards life, he replied that he thought humility was all right as an attitude toward life, but never toward the camera. Anyway, he insisted, he does not like definitions. He does not approve of them as helpful

Labels belong on luggage as far as I'm concerned; they don't mean anything in art.
—Fellini (Budgen, *Fellini*, p. 92)

You can photograph anything and everything at random. This is the reason for the chaos, in my belief. . . . totally ungifted people who, without the advent of this theory about the presentation of reality in the most objective manner possible with no intervention from outside, would probably only have felt themselves called to give lectures, ventured on filming their own presentations of reality with such humility that everyone was bored to tears.
—Fellini (Budgen, p. 92)

For me the principal effort is to create an atmosphere in which the film can be born with the greatest spontaneity without being forced to remain within the limits or in the path of the

at all in dealing with what happens. What takes place and what it says about reality, that is the issue, and in the process of determining this, attempting definitions is only a confusion, not helpful at all.

To go back to Rossellini: he said that to manipulate, to stage, to decide on what would be filmed before focusing in with the camera was to act the role of God. He wants to be free of any such role—no God-playing for him. That is the main problem with the world today—people who are in a position to do it are busy doing what is God's job. Rossellini even questions calling himself an artist. It is an outmoded concept, he says. The artist manipulates the world. Rossellini only wants to record it. That is enough. To show it as it is.

With this point of view Fellini disagrees completely. He is self-consciously the artist. He does plan, manipulate, arrange. He works feverishly in planning a scene for a film. Sets are lavishly designed and built, or the whole shooting company is transported to a location scene—and then there is more construction. Lights must be right. Great care is given to cosmetics. The actors are lived with, talked with, cajoled, threatened, rehearsed. And then the shooting may go on and on into the night, with the people involved drooping, limping, cursing. Money is spent, more money, just so that Fellini can get the film to be what he wants it to be.

Actually, he seldom knows in advance exactly what it is he really wants. His skill is in recognizing when he meets it. He makes all kinds of elaborate preparations. The scenario is written, re-written, and amended. And then he is liable to improvise. Only he, the director,

knows what is right. There is no lack of planning. But the essential is improvisation.

This is not as paradoxical as it seems. While
writing this, I chatted with a neighbor, a
prominent neurosurgeon. He told me about
some of his surgeon friends who plan opera-
tions with every move detailed, every piece of
equipment lined up for use at a precise point
in the operation. And when things go according to the plan, all is well. But if they hit the
unexpected, they tend to be immobilized.

My friend says he makes just as detailed
and thorough plans. But often when he gets
into the operation, for example, a spinal
tumor, the situation may be quite different
from what the x-rays had indicated. Should he
follow impulse and close the incision, saying
nothing could be done? No, he revises the plan
and does the operation, which has turned out
to be something quite different from the
expected. Which is the difference between one
who knows the art of surgery and the mere
practicing surgeon.

For Fellini, the film is in the shooting. It is
when the cameras start and the action is under
way that he really begins to know the film
itself. Although there are references to scripts
and screenplays for his movies and among the
credits of film there is usually one labelled
"script girl," what he works from is a scenario. It is quite different from a script or
play.

In the conventional play script, the progression is simply from beginning to end. Dialogue
cues follow immediately upon each other, and
scenes follow one another in predetermined
sequence. A film scenario is designed to be
used in clusters. Scenes are filmed with no

imagination that has
given birth to it. I
am accused of being
an improvisor. It's
not true. I should
say, rather, that
there is in me a con-
stant openness to
ideas, to changes, to
improvements that
may be born less
out of myself than
out of the situation
that is created
around the film and
in which the film
lives and takes form.
   —Fellini (Kast, p.
181)

relation to the continuity they may have in the finished film. Once on a certain set, that set is used up, no matter where it may be located. Actors come and go, often without any comprehension of their contribution to the finished work. The movement is in and out, forward and backward, the tempo constantly changing. Some scenes work out just right on the first take, others have to be done and redone, and some never come off and are discarded.

For Fellini, people and faces are very important. They often determine what the movement of the film becomes. Like Ingmar Bergman, he needs and develops relationships with a company of people, from technicians to actors. They are integral to a film's growth. The names of these people occur on the credit of film after film.

Fellini likes to start with faces. Often the people to whom they belong have no acting or motion-picture experience. Butchers, carpenters, welders—the thing is the face. From the face comes the scene.

He develops an intuitive understanding with these people. He likes to work on the musical sound with composer Mino Rota, for example, because Rota senses what is required and does it. He does not have to have everything explained to him. He knows mostly because he has developed that sensitizing relationship with Fellini required for such a group effort as a great movie.

The other contemporary filmmaker who compares with Fellini is Bergman. In fact, his company is even tighter than Fellini's. During the finishing work of *Satyricon*, both directors were thinking of collaborating on a film.

This somehow has not worked out, although each claims that the other is the film director he most respects. Apparently their egos and styles were not able to blend—perhaps for the very reason that personal relationship with others is necessary to the filmmaking of each. They just did not have the time nor the opportunity to feel with each other beneath the level of ideas. The cognitive level for both artists is important, but by no means enough to sustain a working relationship.

One hopes that their works will never get that peremptory tag "documents of our time." True, they are works that could have been made in no other time but ours. But they are essentially works of art, not documents. Social scientists, etc. may find some clues to the ethos of the sixties by reviewing *La Dolce Vita, Temptation of Dr. Antonio, 8½, Juliet of the Spirits,* and *Fellini's Satyricon.* But they will never really care, nor understand, unless they can see and know them as art.

Rossellini is quite right in noting that to treat film as art is to assume something of a god-like posture. God is Creator. He makes things and he also makes them new. God does it in his universe, in his world. It was given man to have been made in his image. The essential clue to the God-man relationship is creativity. Creativity is not passive. It must work at new possibilities and combinations.

What is to be feared is not the artist doing motion pictures in which we see ourselves identified and in which our possibilities and sins are revealed. What is to be feared is a fear of the innovative. This fear of the new, of the radically discontinuous, is what is so often

To give virginity back to Roman orgies is almost a desperate undertaking.
—Fellini (Zanelli, p. 14)

exposed in Fellini films. To freeze the image, to relish stasis is the horrible danger. . . . Death!

Religion, church, decadence, renewal

Fellini's films often deal with the church by odd mixtures of satire, irony, and love. Probably there is no other way for a modern Italian artist to do it. His patronage, unlike Michangelo's, has nothing to do with the church except tangentially—that is, it might try to censor the film. Yet wherever he has gone he has been fronted with its images and persons. And these images are in themselves so powerful, so varied, so wonderfully visual that they have inevitably had an impact on his own sense of reality. His childhood, surely reflected in *8½*, was bent by the church. He says he did not run away from home to join a circus as a little boy; he ran away from the school run by Clarissimi priests, who operated with the boys from a medieval basis of rewards and punishments—mostly punishment.

Yet the films of Fellini indicate that he must be profoundly religious. It would have taken a person immersed in Christian myth to have scripted *The Miracle*, which roused the wrath of such an aggressive institutionalist as Cardinal Spellman. His approach to the creative act makes sense when related to the basic Christian doctrine of Creation. He does not have to state the doctrine of the Incarnation in words—time and again his films illuminate it.

When the church comes off badly, it seems to deserve such treatment. The church of his films is for the most part the church of pre-

Vatican II days. The church which is so
important to Dr. Antonio is huge and nearly
empty. The ordinary priests, however, are out
where they ought to be—where the people are.
The important ecclesiastic in *8½* is like
Antonio's building—empty. He is quite outside and irrelevant to the world where people
live and work. Guido is in need, and so are
others, who want him to intercede with the
Cardinal for them. Guido is granted an interview, but when he arrives to talk, the Cardinal
is in another room, wrapped in steam and
towels. Guido can make contact with the fog
only through a little window. The ecclesiastical counsels come muffled in Latin and doctrinal generalizations. Guido cannot hear
much of it and cannot understand what he
does hear. Soon even the window is closed.
No help for Guido's unhappiness from that
quarter.

While the closing scene from *The White
Sheik* finds the distraught newlyweds being
hurried into a general papal audience, formal
and conventional and not at all meeting their
needs, in *La Strada* the church's representatives are closer to the people. This ought to
be, for *La Strada* deals in love and innocence,
which is what the Gospel is about. Love is a
force and a mystery, with a strength to do
battle with brutality, with indifference. The
convent and church in *La Strada* are strong
and real, and Gelsomina feels the presence,
even as she will go on the road in her buffet-
ing journey with Zampano. In her time in the
convent, Gelsomina feels herself to be whole
as a person. She finds strength in the church.
There is nothing rational nor intellectual
about it. It is as elemental as fire and water.

UNCLE: Come on,
everybody walk
faster.
*(The group hurries
toward the long pro-
cession of newly-
weds which is near-
ing the doors of the
basilica.
Superimposed on an
overall image of the
sundrenched piazza,
with the facade of
St. Peter's and the
procession climbing
the steps up to the
doors, and the stat-
ue of the angel atop
the colonnade.)*
—*The White Sheik*

GELSOMINA: With
your spouse, I with
mind.
—talking to nun in
La Strada

FAUSTO *(smiling)*:
An angel. Made out
of solid wood. It's
been in our house
but we have to sell
it now. . . . It's a
real bargain. *(The
appearance of the
angel in the sack
catches the nun un-
prepared. She comes
out to examine the*

rosy face and blue eyes of the statue, then turns to look at the two friends once more with growing suspicion. Her eyes also reveal a mute, shocked reproof for this disrespectful way of carrying angels around. Giudizio suddenly erupts with an undignified yell.)
GIUDIZIO *(rapidly)*: Angel, angel, angel, angel! . . . *(The nun starts in fear. She backs toward the door.)*

NUN: No, we've already got lots of angels. . . . Good-bye.
—I Vitelloni (pp. 87-88)

But for Guido in *8½* it is a different world, and the church is not capable of responding to the need of such a guilt-ridden, lost man. For the sophisticate there is no point of contact with the church. It says nothing that has any relevance to Guido's problem.

In *I Vitelloni*, whether it is the monk up a tree or a nun at a convent door, there is irrelevance to the rest of the world, but there is also both firmness and strength. The monk and the nun are delightful, real persons. But they are in a different orbit.

The Nights of Cabiria, which follows *La Strada* and also utilizes Giulietta Masina, may be the most humanly compassionate of Fellini's works. Fr. Giovanni is Cabiria's firm friend, a good man, working hard among the poor people of his parish. He is never judgmental in his relationship with the prostitute. He tries to encourage her to live a different life, but it is always Cabiria as a person to whom he is related. The church's miracle is a fiasco, and deservedly so, for it could hardly have been managed as commercial exploitation. In contrast, the person of the priest is real. He serves where there is need.

The same split between an institution exploiting religious needs by elaborate and sentimental staging while various priests and nuns do minister with compassion is integral to *La Dolce Vita*. In both *La Dolce Vita* and *8½* the priestly garb is put on by women. Sylvia in *La Dolce Vita* has a moment of luminous transformation, and her sprinkling of Marcello's head (a baptism) is beautiful. The women as priests in *8½* succeed in turning them into nonhumans, abstractions.

However it is that Fellini deals with religious imagery, it is always lurking about in his films. Without doubt religion is much at the center of his vision. All of his films are immersed in the questions of personhood, of being alive, of responding to need and giving love. Intrinsically their pulse is that of religion. *Satyricon* is the most religiously potent of them all. Fellini attempts an amazing *tour de force*, namely an answer to the question, What is a world like without Christ? Fellini invents another world, elusive as colors through stained glass, bloody as an abattoir, sterile as a moonscape, ambiguous as the Delphic oracle, decipherable as a medieval palimpsest.

Satyricon has a story to tell, but the narrative line is fragmentary, disconnected. In literary terms it is a bit like the picaresque, but it is filmic rather than literary. It is dreamlike strange in color and incident, and yet it mysteriously hangs together. The passion and the faces, surroundings, gestures, walls, and banquets are invented, imagined.

Fellini felt he needed to destroy our myths of antiquity, the "clean" ancient world of serene temples and classic statuary. Could such an image possibly be compatible with people paying their way into Madison Square Garden to eat nuts and joke with one another as they watched people die?—seventy-five pairs of gladiators red in an afternoon of entertainment? In place of the fantasy of a romanticized Rome, he gives us an ancient world "seen through the fears of man today."

As Moravia told Fellini, the film suggests Dante's *Inferno*. "All these monsters, whether hideous or beautiful, that you've crammed into your film, all these albino hermaphro-

Agony as a spectacle comes to an end in history with the coming of Christianity. But let's go back to your sense of alienation.
—Moravia, in conversation with Fellini (Zanelli, p. 26)

Satyricon is a psychedelic movie, historical science-fiction, a journey into time, a planetary world, away from our everyday logic and rhythm; counterimages, counterdialogue.
—Zanelli (p. 35)

I tried to look at pagan Rome with eyes not obscured by the myths and ideologies that have succeeded each other throughout two thousand years of history. Now to find myself compared to the primitive Christian seems rather queer.
—Fellini, in conversation with Moravia (Zanelli, p. 30)

dites, these hairy dwarfs, these elephantine
prostitutes, these lascivious Gitons, these para-
lytic, maimed, dropsical, truncated, blind,
halt, and lame etcetera people, reveal, besides
your own Baroque temperament with its in-
clination to wildly unrestrained imagination,
the idea that antiquity signified nature without soul, sunk in the depths of irremedial
corruption.

"In fact the monster exemplifies corruption
not of the spirit but of the body; not moral, but
physical putrefaction." (Moravia 29) It is,
Moravia insisted, a non-mural inferno, without
purgatory, certainly without paradise.

It could, of course, be suggested that three-
fifths of those who read Dante get through
the *Inferno* and never read the latter two
parts. Or, we might also insist that the Christian story is not complete without the resur-
rection. But is it not also perverted without
the Crucifixion?

In any case, Fellini attempts no *Summa*,
nor should he be rebuked because he has not.
He has not even attempted a prologue, though
he does, in fact, produce one. But it is film,
not theology; art, not exposition. He illumi-
nates and reveals. He leaves the "meaning" to
us.

Satyricon is the imagination's world, without Christ. Set the imagination going . . . How
does the world *with* Christ?

The originality of film "is almost impal-
pable, and extremely difficult to reach, since a
film is above all a journey, which fatally creates bonds between actor and spectator."

Bibliography

Boyer, Deena. *The Two Hundred Days of 8½,* trans. Charles Lam Markmann. The Macmillan Company, N.Y., 1964.

Budgen, Suzanne, *Fellini.* The B.F.I. Education Dept., London, England, 1966. (Includes an interview with Fellini that appeared on Belgian television.)

Fellini, Federico. *Fellini's Satyricon,* ed. Dario Zanelli and trans. Eugene Walter and John Matthews. Ballantine Books, New York, 1970. (Includes a dialogue between Alberto Moravia and Federico Fellini, scriptwriter Bernardino Zapponi's account of his relationship with Fellini, and the screenplay.)

——. *Juliet of the Spirits,* ed. Tullio Kerich, trans. Howard Greenfield. Ballantine Books, New York, 1965. (Includes a transcription of the screenplay and Kerich's interview with Fellini.)

——. *Variety Lights* and *The White Sheik,* screenplays trans. Judith Green. Grossman Publishers, New York, 1971.

——. *I Vitelloni, Il Bidone, The Temptations of Dr. Antonio,* screenplays trans. Judith Green. Grossman Publishers, New York, 1970.

Sarris, Andrew. *Interviews with Film Directors.* Discus Books, Avon, New York, 1967. (The interview with Fellini by Pierre Kast appeared originally in *Cahiers du Cinema,* Mar. 1965, trans. Rose Kaplin.

Taylor, John Russell. *Cinema Eye, Cinema Ear: Some Key Film-Makers of the Sixties.* Hill and Wang, New York, 1964.

LUIS BUNUEL
AND THE DEATH OF GOD

Peter P. Schillaci

Introduction

*I intend to show with a cold, white eye what they have
done here on earth in the name of God.*

—Luis Bunuel, Filmmaker

Only the Christian can experience the death of God.

—Thomas Altizer, Theologian

A young woman sits on a balcony, enjoying the cool
night air. A man steps out behind her, and as a cloud
passes across the moon, he bends over and with a straight
razor slits her eye in dramatic closeup. The man with the
razor is Luis Bunuel, and the film is his first, *Un Chien
Andalou (The Andalusian Dog)*.

The image just described makes an indelible impression, and its impact derives from associations that outlive
the trauma of each viewing. D. W. Griffith spoke for all
filmmakers when he said, "What I am trying to do, above
all, is to make you see." Through forty years of filmmaking, Luis Bunuel has been opening our eyes to see
what might otherwise evade our notice. And he is not
averse to using a razor slash where it is appropriate.
Images of blindness and vision can be found in most of
his works. In fact, the Bunuel films notorious for their
deformed humanity—their cripples, dwarfs, diseased, and
mutilated—savor an image that recurs more often than
any other, the blind man. His visage is the face of Bunuel
himself.

The personal dimension in each Bunuel film converts

111

the body of his work into a mosaic of the man. But the price he has paid to maintain an individual stamp on his films has been great. He has been censored, brought to trial, banished, and exiled many times. In bad times he has been willing to accept almost any commission so long as it gave him the freedom to make films. Only in good times could that freedom be called artistic. And yet, even in those films where he was least free, he seems never to have surrendered his personal vision. Perhaps this is why Luis Bunuel never refers to himself as an artist, and in spite of his cruel experiences never theorizes on the role of the creator in a society.

Bunuel's critics have cast him in enough roles to fill a dozen lives, but he manages to evade each category imposed upon him. To some, his Spanish temperament, with its supposed predilection for anarchy and tragic death, is enough to explain the man. For others, he is the iconoclast par excellence, an ally against a host of enemies, but one who never reveals his own allegiances. Early critics were content to dismiss him as a surrealist madman, while later analysts could put him down as a perennial atheist, indefatigably marking the screen with his pornographic theological anagrams. And finally, when writers were unable to discover his political credo, he became an "anarchist," socially, morally, artistically, and religiously destructive of all values and principles.

It is customary, after cataloging mistaken judgments on Bunuel, to make one's own definitive critique, a categorical imperative designed to fall on both subject and reader alike, capturing once and for all the elusive spirit of the man. This is not the intention of the present work. Without subscribing to (or negating) any of the previous judgments, I would like to introduce a somewhat neglected facet of Bunuel's work. It is an interesting correlation between Bunuel's filmic vision and a recent trend in theology. Whatever else he has done, Luis Bunuel has consistently demythologized a vestigially Christian culture, and he has done so since long before theologians announced that God is dead. He has gone from avant-garde visual theatrics to a bland, straightforward directorial style, all the time nourishing the same obsession—to lay to rest all the myths, secular and religious, which diminish man's freedom. That he has done so almost benevolently in recent films is simply part of the paradox of a director whose vision has made him one of the most important filmmakers in the history of cinema.

There is no way to "prove" Bunuel's demythologizing role. But the idea can be made plausible and even informative if we can develop it out of his remarkable films, rather than out of a theological context. One could cite several recent works which approach films as theological tracts, and which dissect a director's works according to the surgical procedures of literary analysis. The worst of such writings callously impose speculative categories on films, tyrannizing them with an elaborate theological taxonomy. The best of the failures can do little more than discuss the action and dialogue of the films, as if they were not primarily a dynamic combination of images and sounds. In order to avoid the more gross errors, we will first treat representative selections from among Bunuel's works, organizing them as parts of an evolving creative vision. Then, after presenting the works *as film*, we can proceed through the surrealist imagery and visual metaphors of the filmmaker into the theological areas suggested by each film.

Every good film exists on many levels. However, it is characteristic of Bunuel's work that the contents of its subconscious core of meaning can only be suggested. His images, like fragments of a dream, invite a sensitive reflection on the psyche that produced them. There is, of course, an obligation to defend, at each step, this descent from the surfaces of a film into depths that are ultimately theological. But it is my contention that beneath the naive anticlericalism, the early iconoclasm, and the benign disbelief of his films, there exists a consciousness too perceptive of the sacred to warrant a facile categorization as "atheistic." This is not to canonize Bunuel as a secular saint and therefore "one of us." Rather, it is to suggest that he is a fully human, creative artist, fascinated with human problems and more than normally preoccupied with the work that came to be called "demythologizing." Our investigation may lead to the conviction that Bunuel is actually mourning the God who abandoned him by "dying," by becoming that name used to justify the horrors he most detests. But if the reader is so convinced, I hope that it will be as a result of our analysis of the films of Bunuel, rather than at the insistence of our argumentation.

1

The Golden Age

The screen is a dangerous and wonderful instrument, if a free spirit uses it. It is the superior way of expressing the world of dreams, emotions and instinct. The cinema seems to have been invented for the expression of the subconscious, so profoundly is it rooted in poetry. Nevertheless, it almost never pursues these ends.

—Luis Bunuel[1]

Some famous men seem never to have had a childhood. Bunuel is one of these men. His personality is so clear and forceful that we find it difficult to imagine a time when it was not fully operative. But there is another reason why it is difficult to approach Bunuel's childhood. Our minds are filled with the grim images of Bunuel's children, those whom he conceived in his imagination as threatening, sexually precocious, faintly evil. They seem never to have known the romantic innocence of Wordsworth's recollections. They are likely to have tipped over an amputee's cart, or tripped a blindman *(Los Olvidados)*, or to have jumped rope with the cord used in a hanging suicide *(Viridiana)*. One expects, then, to find that Bunuel's

1. Direct quotes from Luis Bunuel are difficult to attribute, and almost impossible to authenticate. The majority of quotes cited in this work are taken from Raymond Durgnat, *Luis Bunuel* (Berkeley: University of California), 1968, or translated from Ado Kyrou, *Luis Bunuel* (Paris: Editions Seghers), 1963.

childhood was a nightmare of deprivation and horror. But from all appearances his family of landowners in Calandra, Spain, provided for all his needs, including love. Bunuel was sent to a Jesuit college—almost a stock element in the past of Catholic critics of religion—which apparently provided him with a permanent theological imagination. Little is known of his parents or his relations with them, but his reputation as a pious and studious child indicates that they may have regulated his life rather closely. Whether one surmises that this was a climate of love or of repression depends largely on how we interpret the autobiographical events in Bunuel's films.

Although it is a period never adequately explored, Bunuel's years at the famous Residencia de Estudiantes in Madrid were extremely important, bringing him as they did into close friendship with a remarkable group that included philosopher Jose Ortega y Gasset, poet Federico Garcia Lorca (equally famed for his role in the Spanish Civil War), and perhaps most important of all, Salvador Dali.

This was Bunuel's background, and it prepared him for his Golden Age, a notion treated with crushing irony in the title of his second film, L'Age d'Or. Dabbling in acting and directing, the young Bunuel was soon drawn to film, founding one of the first European film clubs at the University of Madrid in 1920. He took his degree in philosophy and letters, then followed the pilgrimage of intellectuals to Paris, where film was just beginning to be taken seriously. This was the period of the French Impressionists and of Picasso, a time in which photography was helping painters like Renoir to discover light, and in which painters such as Fernand Leger worked in film (Ballet Mecanique, 1924). Gertrude Stein was collecting Impressionist paintings, entertaining creative people, and learning to do with words what the Cubists were doing with images. The cinema had already taken off in two directions: the journalistic actuality of the Lumiere brothers, and the poetic fantasy of the visual magician, Melies. This dualism was to appear as an unresolved tension in the works of Luis Bunuel. As a young film-maker he worked as assistant to Jean Epstein, collaborating on such films as *La Chute de la Maison Usher*, a significant introduction to the Poe cult of the period. When with characteristic independence he decided he had learned enough, Bunuel refused an attractive offer to work under Abel Gance and instead went off to Spain with Salvador Dali. When they returned, Bunuel had in hand what was, in effect, the script of *Un Chien Andalou*.[2]

It took Bunuel only a short time to discover his life work. In four years, and in three very different films, he formulated the cinematic vision that would last a life-time. His first works were at once heavy with pessimistic irony and alive with youthful energy. *Un Chien Andalou* appeared in 1928 as the beginning of a career of experimentation in surrealist forms. The next year, *L'Age d'Or* savagely inaugurated Bunuel's long campaign of demythologizing religion. And in 1932 *Las Hurdes (Land Without Bread)* committed Bunuel to a style of social outrage masked as documentary reportage. These were diverse elements, mixed even in the three films cited, but they would soon blend into a unity of subject matter and style, of image and vision, so complete as to be insepara-ble. Only naive observers would thereafter feel compelled to classify subsequent films rigidly in one category or another.

The opening title of *Un Chien Andalou* is a fairytale preface "Once upon a time . . . ", but it would be futile to expect the seventeen-minute film to tell a story. On its most basic level, it is intended to destroy narrative logic, among other things. The surrealist school, in film as in art, tried to release the contents of the subconscious

---

2. Early biographical details have been taken from several sources. This material was derived from John Russell Taylor, *Cinema Eye, Cinema Ear* (New York: Hill and Wang, 1964), pp. 83-85.

through free association and the expression of pure feelings in images. The result was a film consisting in a series
of unrelated scenes, images that seemed to have been
joined in a dream rather than in a shooting script.

After the brutal razor slash of the eye, described
above, the chronologically nonsensical title "Eight years
later . . . " introduces an effeminate young man cycling
down the Paris street where the girl lives. As she watches
she is resentful, then compassionate, rushing down to
embrace him protectively when he falls. There follows a
series of bizarre interactions between the two in her
apartment, most of them representing frustrated sexuality. The camera leaves the room at one point to peer
down on a street scene. A mannish woman is abstractedly
poking a severed human hand with a cane, as police hold
back a curious and horrified crowd. The woman is subsequently struck down by a car, an event that seems to be
the stimulus for the cyclist's embarking on a series of
sexual pursuits, one more outrageous than the other. Sex
turns to violence when in a dreamlike episode the cyclist
kills a domineering man who disciplines him like a schoolboy. His death occurs in a park, where casual passersby
witness it and then move on. The action returns to the
apartment, where, outraged by sexual ploys, the woman
leaves, stepping directly onto a seashore where yet another young man impatiently awaits her. Walking along
the rocky shore, they find the cyclist's clothing and the
box in which the severed hand had been placed. Under a
last title, "In the Springtime . . . ", the camera discovers
the couple buried up to their waists in the sand, dead.

The life of *Un Chien Andalou* is found, not in the
above catalog of actions and images, but in the shocking
and provocative associations it freely creates and breaks.
The film confirms Bunuel's contention that cinema is
"the superior way of expressing the world of dreams,
emotions and instincts." The ironic titles highlight a
shattered chronology, refuting causal sequence or motiva-
tional rationale for the film's actions and transitions.

Characters do not unify the experience. They are all marked by an ambiguous sexuality—effeminate men and mannish women—but they are inconsistent even within these categories. The abrupt and exaggerated eruptions of emotion strike the contemporary viewer as ludicrous, but they are clearly related to the perverse sexuality which rejects any expressive control of the passions. The young man is spurred into lechery apparently by the violent auto accident; the girl stands still for fondling, but then defends her person vigorously; the man, in turn, becomes less spontaneous. In one of the most remarkable scenes in any of Bunuel's films, the cyclist goes into a frenzy, kicks aside the furniture, and, seizing two ropes, pulls an incredible pile of debris, driftwood, two startled clerics, and a pair of grand pianos decorated with suppurating dead donkeys toward the girl. It is an unforgettable image of the dead weight of the past, the burden of the repressed contents of his psyche.

The dreamlike quality of the film is a function not only of the rejection of waking logic, but of the casual way it presents the most bizarre disjunctions. At times, as in the dying fall of the domineering man, the dream fantasy becomes poetic, beginning in the apartment and ending in the park, where his hand grazes the naked back of a woman in a statuary pose. At other times, the dream becomes a nightmare of nameless fears, pursuits, and frustrations. Throughout, sexual symbols provide what little associational unity exists among the images. They are a catalog of Freudian metaphors, too complex to analyze in detail.[3] Nevertheless, the recurring castration motif seems to frustrate all hope of "normal" relations between the sexes. The reason is tabus erected by church and society. At each stage of socio-sexual development, training and education intervene to stifle candid expression of the passions: birth, infantile eroticism tied to

3. See Durgnat, pp. 22-37 ("Un Chien Andalou") and pp. 46-55 ("Themes and Variations") for a complete listing of Freudian references.

nursing, masturbatory action (ants in the palm of the hand), sexually discriminatory clothing, schoolboy homosexuality, incestuous longings, sexual role-playing involving aggression, modesty, and "chastity"—each represents a cruel and frustrating repression. The result is perversity, the derivation of sexual pleasure from violence and death, the recurring threat to sexual identity, and worse. The idyll on the beach ends with the couple dead, helplessly exposed to the insects and the elements in their resting place in the sand.

One could hardly describe *Un Chien Andalou* as an underground film in an era that lacked an adequately established cinema from which to depart for shock tactics. But the film was, even in that age of experimental discovery, uniquely original. Five years earlier, in 1924, Rene Clair had filmed *Entr'acte*. It was, if anything, more spontaneously associational than *Un Chien Andalou*, full of visual ambiguities which created interest. A ballerina's legs and toutou, seen through glass from below, make her leaps look like the rhythmic open and close of a flower. But when the camera searches out "her" face it proves to be a man's bearded countenance. In the strongly philosophical/political circle of the Paris surrealists, *Un Chien Andalou* was the ticket admitting Bunuel and Dali to membership. In fact, even the Paris intelligentsia at large accepted *Un Chien Andalou* as a delicious scandal, which it was. Like an insult that compliments its victim, the film assumes we will recognize a subtle affront. But the radically different ways in which Bunuel and Dali accepted this "liberal" reception underlined their opposite temperaments and foretold the end to a collaboration that was improbable from the start. Today, often in defense of Bunuel's "auteurship," it is common to deemphasize Dali's role in this film and in *L'Age d'Or*, which followed two years later. The issue of crediting this unusual collaboration may never be resolved. It seems clear that while Dali worked into the script elements later recognizable in his canvases, he had relatively little to do

with the making of the film itself.[4] On the other hand,
Bunuel learned from showman Dali that shock tactics
only earn the confining embrace of the overcultured, a
following that clamors for ever more potent charges of
creative electricity. Dali responded as a showman and
became one of the contemporary school of theatrical
artists, spending as much energy on creation as on the
placing of his oversized signature on his works. Bunuel,
on the other hand, took the road of obscurity, an artistic
anonymity which became a kind of burial, then exploded
into a series of the most personal films ever made.

Although Dali's influence diminished in *L'Age d'Or*,
Bunuel continued to experiment in the surrealist style,
focusing this time more directly on the fortress of established religion. *L'Age d'Or* is a story of frustrated love in
a repressive religious setting. The Majorcans, a mysterious
group, are attempting to found a New Rome on a rocky
island. An earlier group of bishops in full religious garb
had been seen celebrating mass, but they have long since
been reduced to mitred skeletons. The new arrivals are
interrupted in the midst of the inaugural ceremony by
the cries of two lovers passionately embracing on the
ground. They are separated, and the man is jailed while
the woman is released. He escapes to rejoin his love at a
bizarre society reception at which the orchestra is playing
themes from Wagner's *Tristan and Isolde.* Their attempts
to consummate their love are interrupted by phone calls,
the woman's father, and by their own inhibitions. Infuri-
ated, the man dashes into the house to throw half the
furnishings out the window. The action breaks here,
taking us to the Castle of Selligny (as the title says) where
a scene from De Sade's *Les 120 Journees de Sodome* is
being enacted. The film ends with a shot of a puzzling
symbolic cross.

As in the case of Bunuel's first film, this gross action
tells us little about *L'Age d'Or.* But if we turn to another

4. *Cinema Eye, Cinema Ear,* p. 85, argues this point persuasively.

level of images, a pattern of relationships emerges. The opening scene is a nature documentary on scorpions, and its juxtaposition with the religious ceremony seems designed to connect the two. The film itself is a scorpion, as Raymond Durgnat observes, with "five articulations, in the last of which the venom is concealed."[5] The only sympathetic characters are a ragged band of guerrillas who try to oppose the Majorcan invasion. But the slaves of tradition, tipping their hats to the skeletal hierarchy, move to set up a New Rome which places the ship of St. Peter literally "on the rocks." The separation of the lovers is not a mere distraction, but the very premise of the new religious society. The couple represents *amour fou*, the mad, single-minded passion which Bunuel uses to symbolize the natural man, unfettered by time and space, tabu or custom. The Church's frustration of the natural man is its demise.

But the lovers are not themselves free from the corruption which pervades the society. The girl, Lya Lys, returns home to find a giant cow on her bed; the man, Gaston Modot, is marched by police through "Imperial Rome," a place of revolution and destruction. Each fantasizes about the other—he, stimulated by perfume and stocking advertisements, she, sitting at her mirror, buffing her nails. The result is an episode of erotic longing whose mood is ironically accompanied by clanging cow bells. The social reception is a stage for Bunuellian absurdities. The lover sneaks in with a certificate of social importance which the hypocritical society recognizes. His monomaniacal search for his love is interrupted when her mother spills wine on him and sends him into a rage that culminates in his slapping her face. In the midst of all this, a giant oxcart loaded with drinking peasants trundles through the hall, completely unnoticed by the guests. A fire breaks out in the kitchen, killing one of the maids, but again, little notice is taken. Outside, a gamekeeper,

5. Durgnat, p. 38.

annoyed by his Mongoloid son, takes a gun and shoots him dead. High society, it seems clear, is indifferent to the violence, death, and social destruction, even when this monster created by itself turns on it to destroy the society. Modot's slap is more of a *cause scandale* than the oxcart, fire, or casual murder.

A garden concert appears to give the lovers their chance, but they are frustrated in every way. They seem riveted in their chairs, and a male statue's white feet distract Modot from his love-making. He is called to the phone for a scolding by his boss, the Minister of Good Works, but seems unmoved by the news that his dereliction has caused millions of deaths. In fact, he tells the man to "drop dead," whereupon the Minister does so, his body rising to the ceiling, allowing the camera to establish continuity between his feet and the statue toes, which Lya Lys is now sucking. The couple's resumed love-making is interrupted by her father, a concertmaster who has left his orchestra with a migraine. Lya Lys' comforting kiss becomes a passionate embrace of her father, and Modot, enraged, races into the house. Out the window come the symbols of his repression: a long-yoke plow, a stuffed giraffe, and two bishops complete with crozier, plus a burning Christmas tree. These are sexual symbols which parallel those dragged by the cyclist in *Un Chien Andalou*.

The ending of the film shows that Bunuel's associational unity is more in control than in his first film. His surrealist style seems to have matured, a factor which some attribute to Dali's diminished collaboration, others to the introduction of sound. Bunuel shows a remarkable mastery of the new cinematic instrument. Almost every modern device for reinforcing images with sound can be detected in *L'Age d'Or:* deliberate distortions, characters' thoughts presented voice over images, music that is either absurdly out of harmony, or effectively evocative of previous episodes. Even the "story" manifests more continuity, as the frustrated love of Lya Lys and Gaston

Modot encounters the repressive sexuality of the culture. But in spite of all these elements, discontinuity is still the salient feature of the film. The emotional reversals of the couple are bizarre, played at the height of rage or lust, disorienting the viewer. Hints of sexual perversion abound as warped expressions of the simple love *(amour fou)* which the Church denies. The result is incest, foot fetishism, and such deviate sexuality as the De Sade episode's ultimate degeneracy.

The religious comment of *L'Age d'Or*, if one can summarize it, shows the Church shipwrecked on the hard, unyielding rock of human nature. Although the first religious leaders have died, society carries on, building a barren empire based on the denial of the human. The monster of sexuality reappears, but must be repressed by social customs and by their right arm, the police, who serve the rich. The result is a ruling class out of touch with the poor, and with their own emotions. The ultimate victims are the men and women who cannot develop their love. Modot tries throwing out all the phallic substitutes, but to no avail. The logical outcome of Christian sexual morality appears in the tableau of perversity staged by De Sade, in which the Count de Blangis, a murdering sexual orgiast, resembles Christ. The cross in the snow is cold restraint replacing heated passion, and it is decorated not with the body of Christ, but pubic hair. The victim of the crucifixion here is man, nailed to the cross of his human desires. Salvador Dali felt compelled to disown *L'Age d'Or*, complaining in his work *The Secret Life of Salvador Dali* that Catholicism had been attacked "in an obvious way, and quite without poetry." Social and political groups of the time attacked the film and tried to drive it out of Paris, but Bunuel was destined to have his revenge. In the perspective of years, and in the context of a lifetime of films, the critics finally began to note that Bunuel's attack on religion was the work of a skilled surgeon, not an atheist butcher.

Having completed a "fairy tale" *Un Chien Andalou*

and a "nature study," Bunuel might seem to have exhausted the possibilities of surreal fantasy. This, at least, is what critics thought when they reviewed *Las Hurdes (Land Without Bread)* in 1932, and classified it as a departure, Bunuel's first "social documentary." Yet Bunuel refers to it as "one of my surrealist films," and we would do well to listen to him. Under the stylistic formalities of documentary reportage, already familiar from the scorpion sequence of *L'Age d'Or*, Bunuel had discovered a place, a people, a culture in which nature and custom collaborate in a dehumanizing process so complete as to appear surreal.

The Hurdanos live in a mountainous region of Spain so poor as to exceed comprehension. Isolated by the monstrous joke played upon them by the terrain, they live on the verge of starvation, each generation plunging them deeper into near idiocy by interbreeding. Turning to this people, Bunuel trained his camera on horrors he did not have to invent but simply discover. In retrospect, it is apparent that he had already mastered the documentary style, a fact concealed by the surreal, fantastic world of his previous films. The same camera that had gazed unblinking on the absurd in fixed, dispassionate medium shots, now recorded in the same way the horrors of poverty, disease, religious superstition, and voiceless despair. Only a maddeningly objective narration intervenes, and its matter-of-fact description of this Land Without Bread becomes part of the unreal world it portrays. The people are mere insects, or perhaps more like the rats stung by scorpions in the opening sequence of *L'Age d'Or*—abandoned to a level less than human.

Those who described *Las Hurdes* as a deeply concerned social document misread the total consistency of this film with his previous work. There is no pity or outrage on the surface of the film, and yet audiences supplied these ingredients, the stock liberal intellectual response to injustices we are powerless to correct. The revolutionary import of Bunuel's images was veiled by their nonrevolutionary tone. He re-created the cycle of their lives, a downward spiralling nightmare of hopelessness in which each promise of amelioration brought a frustrating deterioration in their condition. Already wasted by malaria, the Hurdanos are driven by hunger to eat fruit before it is ripe, and so they are deprived of any nourishment by dysentery. Too poor to know what bread is, the ignorant peasants bid their children throw away the few loaves given them occasionally by their teachers. But when the teachers respond by making the children eat bread in school, they only set child against parent. Devoid of folklore or art, Las Hurdes nevertheless boasts churches decorated in gold. The schools might conceivably teach those not yet reduced to imbecility by inbreeding, but they are shown to train children to write solemnly such sentiments as "respect the possessions of others." The overall effect of the film is a systematic destruction of hope, made all the more poignant by a history of false aspirations, heartbreaking labors, and discarded projects.

Las Hurdes derives most of its impact from its treatment of the outrageous as completely normal. The camera technique which makes this effect possible is, together with the carefully worded narration, perfectly suited to the subject—conceptual point is masterfully incarnated in concrete images. The village with its surrounding terrain is a visual nightmare, a stone prison without relief—windowless houses, endless stone lanes infested with vipers, and a tiny riverbank where no amount of labor can force the soil to bear fruit. As the camera eye scans the villagers, the narrator notes again and again, "another imbecile." When a burro slips to his death off the narrow trails which are the only contact with the outer world, the futility of the project is marked by the bees, who settle in the dead beast's eyes. The only road to freedom is the river, but the only person we witness taking this route is the body of a small girl, set adrift in an open coffin. It seems superfluous to tax religion with the Hurdanos' condition, but Bunuel notes that the abandoned Carmelite monastery has become a nest of vipers, implying that the new tenants have added nothing new. The viper bite, incidentally, is superstitiously treated with a remedy that proves to be more deadly than the scorpion.

The apparent heartlessness of *Las Hurdes* makes one desperately want to scream, to hear the narrator's flat voice break with emotion, to see the camera's accepting eye close with tears of compassion. But Bunuel's "cold, white eye" will not allow us to enjoy our pity, to indulge ourselves in sympathy. For centuries, the charitable slumming expeditions of church and society have succeeded only in stifling the cry of rebellion in the village, offering hypocritical short-term hope instead of sweeping reforms. Soon the Hurdanos will be unable even to dream that things could be different. For Bunuel, the centuries-old belief that man gained dignity and meaning in suffering is an outrageous lie. Human misery, tolerated because it "brings out the best in people," deleted the need for all but alleviative action. One recalls Flaherty's romantic *Man of Aran*, where the hard environment seemed to forge a superb, self-reliant, courageous people. There is no such consolation for Bunuel's audience, or his subjects. Life for the Hurdanos is according to Hobbes' definition—"solitary, poor, nasty, brutish and short" (a woman of thirty-two looks sixty)—and there is no way out.

It is difficult to convey the agony of disappointment that public acceptance of his films caused Bunuel. *Un Chien Andalou* and *L'Age d'Or* were embraced by those very intellectuals whose values they attacked. *Las Hurdes* was perhaps best understood by the Spanish government, which found it easier to ban the film than to eradicate the problems it uncovered. *Un Chien Andalou* was accepted as the darling, somewhat recherché creation of an eccentric whose company should be cultivated. What was designed as an outrage to every sensibility, a bomb thrown into the midst of every cultural value and aesthetic criterion, a knife pointed at the heart of the Church and related institutions, was enthusiastically assimilated by the cultural elite. Bunuel could only fulminate against the "pack of imbeciles who found beauty or poetry in what is, in essence, nothing less than a desperate, passionate appeal to murder."

Appearing as they did in the infancy of the art, three such films as *Un Chien Andalou, L'Age d'Or*, and *Las Hurdes* should have established Bunuel's reputation and launched a successful career. Instead, the demonstrations touched off by *L'Age d'Or's* caricature of Jesus as a degenerate orgiast forced the film (and its director) underground for over a quarter of a century. In this atmosphere, finances became a problem. Unable to turn to his mother (as for *Un Chien Andalou*), or to a rich patron (the Vicomte de Noailles supported *L'Age d'Or*), or even to a fellow revolutionary (an anarchist friend's 20,000 peseta win in a lottery financed *Las Hurdes*) Bunuel lost his freedom to make films as personal as his first three endeavors. Nevertheless, in this space of four years, from 1928 to 1932, he had completed his basic vision, and it would never fail him again.

These early films are subject to reinterpretation in the light of subsequent Bunuel works, but their consistency with the most important and the most trivial of his large-budget films invites us to reflect on their unity of conception. Bunuel's style had preserved the film version of the surrealist esthetic in a way that no single painting could have done, and yet Bunuel cultivated the form only as a way of looking at reality. His credo was more important than a school of art, and surrealist fantasy was chosen as a way of making his uniquely personal statements effective. The major themes of his lifetime concern had already emerged in their basic outline. The attack on organized religion, the affirmation of a natural humanity seldom given a voice, the fascination with human deformity, perversion, and the capacity for evil—all were there. His iconoclast's hammer was already demolishing statues

and idols, churches and institutions that pretended to
protect but really destroyed men. The emotions of his
films were those of his own life—anger, a lust to live,
direct, passionate expression, and a sense of social outrage. With *Las Hurdes,* his social concern took on cosmic
overtones that transcended the social, political, or religious. Ultimately, Bunuel's vision is metaphysical and
theological. We may look in vain for recognizable elements of these categories in his films, but nevertheless
they are operative in these disciplines, usually reserved to
their own experts. Beyond theories of sin and guilt,
beyond laws and moral codes, Bunuel dramatizes clashes
between good and evil that existed before man was able
to write commentaries about them.

I believe that any critique or evaluation of Bunuel's
work which ignores this cosmic concern cannot do justice
to his creative contributions to film. He himself raises the
issues, and so it is legitimate for us to pursue them
through his insights and beyond. What may surprise us,
however, is that Bunuel proves to be more expert with
the surgeon's scalpel than with the iconoclast's hammer.
To apply the metaphor in the area of religion, Bunuel has
proved interested not so much in the outward shapes as
in the interior organs and nervous system of the institutions on which he operates with such ferocious zeal. Not
every stroke is as brutal and destructive as the razor slash
of *Un Chien Andalou.* Endowed with the natural instinct
of a demythologizer, Bunuel quickly senses the threat to
the human in myths both secular and religious. Threatened critics have often complained that the patient died
in surgery. But Bunuel continues his work, announcing
the Death of God after becoming convinced that God had
never made any discernible difference to the human
exploitation that is man's history.

This "Golden Age" of creativity closes with a statement, an outpouring of rage that Bunuel was then forced
to bank for many years like the fires of a live volcano: "If
only the white eyelid of the screen reflected its proper

light, the universe would go up in flames. But for the
time being, we can sleep in peace . . . the light of the
cinema is conveniently ossified and shackled." During the
following years of obscurity, the white-hot lava erupted
in small, undetected ways. His films, known better in
rumor than experience, were largely attributed to the
flamboyant Dali, and Bunuel became more and more
obscure. The work which he was forced to do in this
limbo of his history may have contributed to the fury of
a man who never doubted the vision which obsessed him.
But it is a characteristic of that obsession that everything,
however noble or trivial, to which he turned his hand in
these years either confirmed his themes directly, or contributed to the skills necessary for presenting his ideas.
This is a period of gestation during which Bunuel stored
his energies until he could continue the great work of
demythologizing which was his vocation, a vocation he
embraced with a zeal ironically labeled "religious."

2

The Evolution of an Anarchist

Bunuel's next years can be considered a period either of exile or of incubation. In any case, he found himself doing things related to film, but not making the films he wished to make. A period of dubbing American films for Paramount in Paris and for Warner Brothers in Spain was followed by film production—four films which he dismisses as of no importance. During the months prior to the Spanish Civil War, he used newsreel footage to make an editing film called *Madrid 36*, part of a series for the Republican Government called *Espana Leal en Armas*. Shortly after this the government collapsed, the Civil War began in earnest, and Bunuel with characteristic pragmatism chose to live in the United States rather than in his native land under Franco. Contacts with American studios seemed to pave the way for an easy transition, and Bunuel came to New York to work at the Museum of Modern Art.

Bunuel's early films remained with him in America like an incubus. When *L'Age d'Or* first appeared, MGM invited him for a brief stay. But now he had been in New York only a short time when his connection with the film caused him to be fired from the Museum. The work he did there—editing Leni Riefenstahl's *Triumph of the Will* into an anti-Nazi film—appears never to have been screened. In 1947, after some dubbing in Hollywood, he received the offer that was to give his career a whole new direction. Bunuel was invited to resume directing in Mexico, a place where he could collaborate with producer Oscar Dancigers, writer Luis Alcoriza, and photographer Gabriel Figueroa. This fruitful environment was to lead to *Los Olvidados*, but before this came a period of exclusively commercial work. Incredible as it may seem, Bunuel made a cheap musical, *Gran Casino*, which is about as ironic as Walt Disney making a sexploitation film. The film was a failure, but it was followed by the successful *El Gran Calavera* (1949). A *calavera* is a wastrel or rogue, and the story involves a drunk millionaire who turns the tables on his moralizing family. When they try to shake him by telling him he's broke, he uncovers their hypocrisy by convincing them, in turn, that he really *is* bankrupt. The film afforded great opportunities for social satire, but Bunuel did not respond, apparently having higher ideological stakes in mind.

Throughout the 1950's, Bunuel made some ten films in which he placed so little of himself that he has dismissed and forgotten them. Overshadowed by *Los Olvidados* and *Nazarin*, these films are almost never seen and so must be treated summarily.[1] Most of them were made in Mexico, where box office appeal meant catering to a fascination with morbid topics such as death, funerals, and wakes. Titles from among these films are sadly symptomatic: *Devil and Flesh* (1950), *Evil Eden* (1956), *Republic of Sin* (1958), and *Island of Shame* (1958). Occasionally the title is more provocative than descriptive, as in the screen version of *Wuthering Heights, Abismos de Passion* (1953). One title does suggest Bunuel's surrealist preoccupation: *Illusion Comes by Bus* (1953).

It would be easy to dismiss other minor films as quickly as these, but a few are close enough to familiar Bunuellian themes to deserve more attention in our

---

1. We are indebted to the books on Bunuel by both Ado Kyrou and Raymond Durgnat for descriptive details on Bunuel's lesser known and seldom seen films.

scrutiny of his evolution as a filmmaker. *El Bruto* (1952), for example, finds Bunuel exploring class struggle, pitting a slaughterhouse worker against a bourgeois boss who melodramatically proves to be his father. Rebellion is the outcome, precipitated by a murder marking the worker's conversion to social reform. This heavy subject was preceded by *Subida al Cielo*, a picaresque comedy in which a young innocent is trying to have a new will drawn up for his dying mother. A bus journey to his lawyer provides a microcosm of the society, and after a number of sexual and other escapades, he returns to his mother (already dead) and his bride-to-be a much wiser man. An episode in this film shows Bunuel once again contrasting joyful natural desire with repressive negations of sexuality. With a woman he meets on the bus, the young man has a night of guilt-free infidelity at a mountain pass which gives the film its name, *Ascent to Heaven*.

Robinson Crusoe (1952) appeared in the same year of frantic productivity, a color film with much higher production values than his other works. It was, to say the least, an unlikely subject for this director. The idea of a moralizing Christian introducing "civilization" to a desert island by reconstructing a model of European culture there seems to contradict all Bunuel's views on social restraint and the natural man.[2] Crusoe, for example, "civilizes" the native Friday by chaining him. However, Bunuel was able to reverse the book's thesis while retaining most of the story's basic action. Instead of triumphing, Crusoe is seen to be crumbling under the pressure of his exile, his elaborate rituals an absurd postponement of madness, and his religious belief useless in enabling him to adapt. The only accretions used to advance this counterthesis are Crusoe's sexual fantasies evoked by women's clothing.

Like *Robinson Crusoe*, *El Bruto* (again 1952) was also a commercial success, especially in Mexico, where it was

2. *Cinema Eye, Cinema Ear*, p. 98.

received as a melodrama on the theme of jealousy. Bunuel apparently had other ideas in mind. The film traces the decline of a devout, moral churchgoer, Francisco, whose passionate obsession for a girl drives him beyond marriage into an insane jealousy that destroys him. The cause is religion, a faith that kept him celibate until past forty, at which time his pent emotions proved too powerful to control, fermenting into a sadomasochistic jealousy. The same man who at the film's beginning assists in Holy Thursday foot-washing ceremonies, is declared criminally insane at the film's end after attempting to strangle a priest. The ties to *L'Age d'Or* are striking, and the film proceeds with a blurring of fantasy and reality in the crazed man's mind executed with surreal virtuosity.

Another study of obsession, treated comically this time, is *La Vida Criminal de Archibaldo de la Cruz* (1955). Archibaldo is the victim of a childhood trauma associating death with desire—so vehement is his boyhood wish for a music box that he thinks this desire has killed his governess. As a man, he tries to confirm this pattern by killing whomever he desires, but each attempt is comically frustrated by his intended victim's natural or accidental death, for which he nevertheless feels guilty. After much mayhem in black comedy style, Archibaldo frees himself by destroying the music box. Bunuel, too, seems freer in this work, introducing only the most casual references to society and religion as the causes of Archibaldo's psychological dilemma.

The film version of *Wuthering Heights* was a project close to Bunuel's major interests and stylistic imagination; the surrealists had always been fascinated with the novel. However, there is little to comment upon in terms of Bunuel's evolution. The only significant alteration made was to have Heathcliff shot to death after breaking into Cathy's grave to embrace her body one more time.

Two films complete the canon of Bunuel's minor works. *La Mort en ce Jardin* (1956) pairs a jungle plane crash and a band of escaped prisoners. Also called *Evil Eden*, this film touches upon the Genesis motif, especially in the macabre spectacle of fugitives dressing in the clothing of the dead. This image, however, is less a religious parody than a reference to class struggle. In *Cela s'Appelle l'Aurore*, the class struggle becomes open revolution. A rich industrialist embodying every virtue that Bunuel detests, rules an island with absolute power, until his brutality provokes the worker Sandro to kill him in revenge for his wife's death. Sandro is driven to suicide, but the revolt continues in the person of his doctor-friend Valerio, who rejects wealth and social acceptance to embrace revolution. The call to bloody rebellion, muffled in Bunuel's early films, here sounds in full cry.

Brief as it is, this survey of lesser films introduces a paradox into our understanding of Luis Bunuel. Interesting for their glimpses of Bunuel's style, his obsessions, his imagery, these films nevertheless repel us by their obvious commercial appeal, their sometimes careless workmanship (most were made in haste), and their ultimately unconvincing arguments. A mass art such as film diminishes a director's freedom to select his properties and treat them honestly in depth. Nevertheless, as the *auteur* theory has so abundantly revealed, commercial directors have managed to place the stamp of their personality and talent on even the most banal films. Bunuel has commented upon this problem as it affects his own career:

> I have always been true to my surrealist principles; the need to eat never excuses the prostituting of one's art. In nineteen or twenty films, I have made three or four which are frankly bad, but in no case have I infringed my moral code. To have a code at all is childish to many people, but not to me. I am against conventional morality, traditional sacred cows, sentimentality and all that moral filth of society which comes into it. Obviously, I have made bad films, but always morally acceptable to me.

It would be interesting to pursue Bunuel's notion of

what is morally acceptable and in line with his moral code. Perhaps he means the ability to impose his vision on a property, even if it requires turning the original around, as he did with *Robinson Crusoe*. At any rate, these films earned him the freedom to make the films that do represent his spirit, even when they proved unprofitable. We had best postpone our judgment on the preservation of his moral code until we examine his more representative works to see if there are traces of erosion in the perverse integrity which he has manifested from his earliest films to the present.

For Bunuel, who was himself a "forgotten one" for so many years, *Los Olvidados* was an appropriate title. When the film appeared in 1950 it seemed to be another neo-realist film, a Mexican *Paisa* in which the wretchedness of the street children stemmed not from war but from poverty. As we shall see, this was a misreading of its intentions. The film's success was worldwide, and it won Bunuel an award for best direction and Gabriel Figueroa an award for best photography at Cannes in 1951. *Los Olvidados* could appeal to a mass audience because it could be understood on several levels—a technique Bunuel had mastered during his years of purely commercial filmmaking. He himself has described it as a film about "social struggle," but this remark must be understood in terms of his own personal vision embodied in the film.

Dramatically, *Los Olvidados* appears to be a melodrama of juvenile delinquency, pitting a good boy against a bad. Pedro is a sympathetic figure, trapped in the street society, unloved by his mother who is abstractly preoccupied with sensual matters. Jaibo enters Pedro's life like a nemesis, teaching him to rob and cheat. But Jaibo's brutal murder of the hard-working Juliano repels Pedro, who takes a job with a silversmith. Pedro's reluctance to inform on Jaibo disappears when he is falsely accused of stealing a silver knife and is sent to reform school. But even there, Pedro cannot escape Jaibo, who robs him of

fifty pesetas a sympathetic official has entrusted to him
for delivery. Pedro now turns and, after revealing that
Jaibo is a murderer, stalks him. But he is no match for
the vicious antagonist and is brutally killed in a friend's
barn. Shortly afterwards, he is revenged when the police
shoot Jaibo to death. Friends discover Pedro's body and,
fearing incrimination, bundle it in a sack and drop it on a
refuse heap, even as Pedro's mother searches for him.

Audiences took *Los Olvidados* for a condemnation of
poverty and ignorance, forcing the film into the familiar
pattern of social comment. But Bunuel's thesis is more
subtle and profound, revolving as it does upon loveless-
ness as the root of misery. Not only does Pedro's mother
refuse him the love he needs, but she ironically becomes
the lover of his murderer. Although Bunuel does not treat
him as evil, the vicious Jaibo seems to personify all that is
bad. But we note that he has never known a father.
Another small boy, Ochitos, is abandoned by his father,
and Juliano is burdened with a drunkard for an old man.
These emotional cripples are tended by a few sympathetic friends and concerned officials, but they cannot be
saved. One by one they must die, unable to live without
love. The most graphic picture of this loveless environment appears in Pedro's dream, the one openly surrealist
touch that Bunuel allows himself in a film that is stylistically documentary. Pedro's appeal for love brings an
erotic response from his mother, then a nightmarish offer
of raw meat, interrupted by the ominous appearance of
Jaibo from under her bed. As a perverse substitute for
familial love, Bunuel surrounds the deprived young with
his usual complement of the deformed and crippled, in
particular one vicious blindman who takes the boys as his
natural enemy. This army of monsters serve as the visible
manifestations of the crippled psyches of the unloved
young ones.

There is a danger in classifying Bunuel's films. They are
works which masterfully confuse fantasy and reality,
purposefully introducing ambiguities into every human

situation, and thereby evading categories. Nevertheless, one can establish meaningful relations among Bunuel's films without necessarily categorizing them, and this is what we shall attempt to do with *Los Olvidados.* The film is the direct heir of *Las Hurdes.* Both of them appear to be social-realist documentaries, but in reality are anguished cries for social upheaval and rebellion. The slender story line of *Los Olvidados,* its mildly sensational flavor, and its power to evoke harmless liberal responses from its audiences, concealed its sting from the critics. At the same time, however, it has the surreal flavor of *Un Chien Andalou,* and a mildly stinging reference to the Church reminiscent of *L'Age d'Or.* These three elements were to blend even more inextricably in two films which for lack of a precedent can only be called reverse morality plays—*Nazarin* and *Viridiana.*

If *Los Olvidados* was a renaissance in Bunuel's career, then *Nazarin* was a secondary explosion. In the eight-year interval between these two films, Bunuel was busy with the minor commercial films we have described earlier: the reversed *Robinson Crusoe* (1952); the call to revolt in *El Bruto* (1952) and in *Cela s'Appelle l'Aurore* (1955); the tragic obsessions of *El* (1952) and the comic foibles of *La Vida Criminal de Archibaldo de la Cruz* (1955); and the allegorical episodes of *Subida al Cielo* (1952) and of *Evil Eden (La Mort en ce Jardin,* 1956). These films, together with age, appear to have drained off the outrage with which Bunuel approached the targets of his own obsessions. Some have interpreted this change as a religious conversion from anguished idealism, through the agonies of agnosticism, into the calm of confirmed atheism. This hypothesis is interesting and merits further examination. Whatever the cause, the two films to follow are different. *Nazarin* and *Viridiana* are occasionally didactic, always ironic, moralities on religion, but they shield their revolutionary concepts in an almost benign deference to the religious institutions which they negate.

Nazarin takes as its eponymous hero one of Bunuel's

most sympathetically drawn characters. The director has admitted that "Nazarin is altogether in my moral line." However, as is the case with any of Bunuel's cryptic remarks, this statement must be examined in the context of the film, where his true feelings toward Nazarin are expressed in images. Nazarin is a worker-priest, living among the poor and sharing all he has with them. He counsels the forlorn Beatrice when her lover has left, and he nurses Andara, wounded in a fight to the death with another prostitute, back to health. Under suspicion from Church and police, Nazarin takes off his clerical garb and pursues his ministry on the road, where his attempts to do good are generally also misunderstood or rejected. Chance brings him to a village where Beatrice and Andara have fled. When he reluctantly agrees to pray over a child near death, a sudden cure convinces them that his sanctity has caused a miracle, and against his orders they follow him, tending to his needs on the road. The three help a village struck by the plague and perform other good works, while at night Nazarin lectures the women on Christian love. However, fate strikes when Beatrice's old lover, Pinto, comes to claim her. The priest and his two companions are arrested and led off in a prison gang, where thieves and criminals torment him over "his women," and blaspheme his calling. Separated from the others, Nazarin is led off alone to ecclesiastical court when, unexpectedly offered a piece of fruit by a roadside vendor, he hesitates, shaken, and then accepts the gift and moves on.

The picaresque journey of *Nazarin* is presented so disinterestedly that many observers were convinced Bunuel had made his most objective comment on Christianity. *La Croix* spoke of the film's "evangelical message," and more than ten years after its completion *Nazarin* was given an award by the National Catholic Office for Motion Pictures, an event that must have afforded Bunuel some wry enjoyment. Nevertheless, the scorpion's sting has not spared the characters in this film. Favorably as Nazarin is drawn, he represents an apparently impossible ideal, since his simple and direct attempt to live the Christ-life only makes things worse. It soon becomes apparent that the women whom he reluctantly allows to follow him have more than a spiritual interest in him. He is abused by the poorest of the poor, the criminals with whom he is imprisoned. At the end, the simple offer of a gift of fruit almost shatters what composure he has left. On the basis of these elements, *L'Humanite* called the film blasphemy, and spoke of its rabid anticlericalism. So much for divergent judgments on Bunuel's films.

Blasphemy or Gospel, *Nazarin* left no audience indifferent, receiving the Grand Prix at Cannes in 1958. Although he had apparently abandoned surrealist shock tactics, Bunuel nevertheless painted a grim picture of Christ's reception in the world today. It may be that his obsession with organized religion was still alive, but that his matured art had driven him into ever more profound critiques of the Church, centering upon its best representatives. This possibility is borne out by his next religious morality play, *Viridiana,* featuring this time a novice in a religious community of women.

Viridiana earned Bunuel another Grand Prix at Cannes in 1961, and is considered by many to be his most perfectly conceived and executed work. Unlike most of Bunuel's films, *Viridiana* emerged from a news item and a series of associations which the director, with Julio Alejandro, developed into a script. Bunuel usually adapts his films from novels and stories. Only four of his feature films—*El Bruto, Los Olvidados, Viridiana,* and *Milky Way*—were written by the director. Although the central character, Viridiana, invites comparison with Nazarin (both are frustrated practitioners of "pure Christianity") they are actually quite different. Viridiana is much more a symbolic character of shadowy motivation, her actions more contrived than were Nazarin's, each of them designed to make a point.

Viridiana is a novice on the eve of final vows, encouraged by her superior to visit her Uncle Jaime, who has supported her education. Reluctantly, she goes to the country estate where he lives with his servant Ramona and her daughter. Don Jaime has never recovered from losing his bride on their wedding night, and Viridiana's resemblance to his wife makes him fall in love with her. But when his offer of marriage is violently rejected, he persuades her to grant one favor—to dress in his wife's wedding finery for their last meal together. In this state, he drugs her, intending to possess her this way, but before he follows his plan, he changes his mind, mortified at his deception. When Viridiana learns what he has done, she leaves in horror, but the police call her back shortly with the news that Don Jaime has hanged himself. Feeling responsible for his death, Viridiana stays on, sharing the mansion with Jorge, her uncle's bastard son, who has inherited the estate and is bent on making it modern and profitable. Viridiana busies herself ministering to a group of beggars whom she houses and directs like a mother superior until, one day, when the owners are in town, the beggars break into the mansion and stage an orgy of eating and drinking. When the masters return, most of the revelers flee, but two remain to overcome Jorge and very nearly rape Viridiana before he can save her. Viridiana now lets down her long hair, puts aside all her religious paraphernalia, and quietly goes to Jorge's room, where she joins him and Ramona (now his mistress) in a game of cards. As rock and roll music blares on a phonograph once reserved for Bach and Handel, the camera draws back farther and farther from the trio.

Viridiana marked Bunuel's return to his native Spain after years of exile, and was the first film he made there since *Las Hurdes.* In spite of his considerable reputation and growing popularity, the script for *Viridiana* had to be submitted to the censors. Bunuel accepted good-humoredly a change in the last scene. But the completed film offended the government more severely than the scenario. This fact may be attributed either to Bunuel's cunning or to his subtlety in making his point. In any case, according to stories, the prints were confiscated and the negative had to be smuggled across the border and printed in France just in time for the film to win its award at Cannes. Whether the film actually encountered this much resistance isn't clear, but at any rate Bunuel had no problem making *The Exterminating Angel* in Spain the very next year.

Why did *Viridiana* shock critics and audiences? The reaction seems to have been less a response to individual scenes than to the film's overall tone of pessimism and surrender. It is true that some of the action, such as the two attempted rapes, gained notoriety from *Viridiana's* status as a novice. But the almost total reversal of values quietly effected by the film seemed to pose a more serious problem. The cultured, music-loving uncle's genteel perversity, his fetishism over his dead bride's clothing, his mad scheme to have Viridiana by force, and his smiling decision to hang himself as a way of keeping her on the estate—none of these sat well with traditional expectations. Furthermore, the blind, the lame, and the halt, who are supposed to become good and holy by Christian example, revert instead to orgy and rapine with no gratitude for favors received. Finally, Viridiana's apparent surrender to the brash, aggressive Jorge at the end seems to signal a personal defeat for one represented as a symbol of established religion. The venom of the scorpion had found its chosen victim with unerring accuracy in the ranks of the religious and governmental establishment.

Bunuel's next film, *The Exterminating Angel*, intensified the attack on Spanish society. Whereas Nazarin and Viridiana were figures in religious dramas, *Exterminating Angel* is an extended metaphor, a parable attacking social conventions with vicious, black humor. Based loosely on a play by Jose Bergamin *(Les Naufrages de la Rue de la Providence)*, the film, reworked by Bunuel and collabora-

tor Luis Alcoriza, became a typical embodiment of the
director's vision.

. A party of rich society people arrive, elegantly dressed,
for an after-theater dinner party. Forebodings of mischief
appear in the sudden, unaccountable departure of the
entire serving staff except the butler. The dinner proceeds
rather well, considering, but when it is time to go, the
guests find they cannot leave the drawing room. One by
one they try, then give up, making themselves comfortable for the night by peeling off formal clothing and lying
on the floor. The next morning, when the butler is
summoned for breakfast, he too is caught in the room's
attraction. The situation persists for days and more. An
elderly man dies, young lovers despairingly take their
lives, and the bodies are stuffed into a closet, another
closet being used as a latrine. Searching for water, the
people uncover a pipe and rip it from the wall. They also
kill and eat some sheep which the hostess had provided
for a joke at the meal. The situation deteriorates until the
guests are about to kill the host, Nobile, whom they
blame for their predicament. Just in time, however, someone suggests they reenact the events leading up to their
paralysis—a device that succeeds in freeing them from
their spell. The disheveled survivors stumble out into the
street, and a few days later attend a *Te Deum* of thanks-
giving at a local church. Each seems to have regained his
composure and dignity lost during his imprisonment, but
when the ceremony is over, the bishop waits for the
congregation to leave, and they wait for him—no one can
quit the church. As the film ends, a flock of sheep is
being driven toward the church doors as its bell tolls.

The Exterminating Angel is a nightmare we have all
experienced in some way, evoking in the viewer a disturbing sense of recognition. It seems obvious that the mansion here is a Freudian place, a set of customs, a life style,
a world view into whose structures people are frozen and
trapped. The people are high society, but the culture and

sophistication (even the courtesy and decency) are apparently only skin deep. In a few days the thin veneer of civilization peels off, people are reminded of their bodies, and are humiliated by their bodily needs. They are forced to find water, slaughter their own meat—in short, to do all the brutalizing things they ordinarily delegate to their slave or servant class. One by one they fall into superstitious rituals, be they Christian, Masonic, or voodoo, and the vices of personal violence, drugs, and philandering emerge. All of this would be bizarre enough, but the extreme sangfroid with which the camera records the horrors makes the film a surreal experience. The evening's conversation has been a barbaric exchange of outrageous insults and allegations, delivered with polite indifference. The disorder of the drawing room soon assaults our senses, its imagined odors seeping under the closet doors to offend us.

Seldom has there been a more savage indictment of "civilization" and its values, and yet, each shock image or sharp word draws a gasp and a stifled laugh typical of black humor's effect. The film's disorder and its over-drawn conceptual points remind us of Bunuel's earliest works. The guests' exodus from the mansion recalls the last sequence of *L'Age d'Or,* when the surfeited orgiasts leave the Chateau de Selligny. The drawing room is an extension of the salon through which an oxcart of singing peasants could pass without notice. And as in *Las Hurdes,* each promise of rescue no sooner appears than it is frustrated and abandoned.

Although his social satires embody a class struggle, Bunuel is seldom drawn directly into a partisan stand. The beggars and derelicts of *Viridiana,* for example, are not pillars of virtue opposed to vicious masters. Nor are the officials of *Los Olvidados* heartless monsters—they try, but are ineffectual. Even where Bunuel prepares a special venom for the rich, as in *The Exterminating Angel,* he manages to portray at least one character on the borderline of the class struggle, who is more attractive than either extreme. These are individuals who have dealt with both camps and developed a survivor's strength. The faithful servants who leave the estate out of disgust over Viridiana's ragged, insolent vagabonds are such characters, as is Ramona herself. The butler in *The Exterminating Angel* is another. Loyal without being obsequious, he lacks the effete hypocrisy of the rich guests and so is able to act when they are paralyzed by apathy or ennui. Perhaps the most striking example of this working-class strength of character appears in Bunuel's next film, *The Diary of a Chambermaid* (1964).

Octave Mirabeau's *Journal d'Une Femme de Chambre* has undergone so many screen transitions (including Jean Renoir's, starring Paulette Goddard, in 1945) that most directors would refuse to approach it. The one advantage Luis Bunuel's film has over the others, however, may be a decisive factor—the casting of Jeanne Moreau in the role of Celestine. The subject matter was, of course, grist for his ideological mill, particularly in his ongoing attack on the establishment.

As chambermaid, Celestine safely navigates through the 1928 household of personal shipwrecks, preserving herself with a mixture of suave deference and open contempt. The Royalist family she serves is close to degeneracy. The neurotic daughter, a feminine hygiene freak, weeps over her husband's philandering with another maid. Her father represents Bunuel's foot fetish obsession, inviting Celestine up to his room to try on some of the dozens of ladies' boots which are his prized possession. Across the way their Republican neighbor hurls insults (and garbage) over the wall separating their properties. The only character who approaches normality is Joseph, the gamekeeper (more sinister than D. H. Lawrence's version), a right-winger who belongs to a semi-fascist group dedicated to straightening out France's morals. When Celestine rightly suspects Joseph of the brutal rape-murder of a small girl she had befriended, she is determined to convict him, even if it means seducing him. But in a peculiar switch, Joseph falls in love with her and moralistically demands that they marry. However, they part violently when she finds evidence of his guilt—evidence that fails, however, to convict him. Discouraged, Celestine accepts marriage with the old Republican officer next door, taking consolation in the cruel practice of making him serve her every wish. Our last sight of Joseph finds him riding the wave of the political future as fascists march through the streets of Paris. It is a typical Bunuel touch that they should shout "Vive Chiappe!" as they pass—Chiappe was the name of the Prefect of Police who, in 1932, led the right-wing fight against *L'Age d'Or*. The scorpion will have his day, after all.

In *Diary of a Chambermaid,* Bunuel once again surveys the nightmare of decadent class privilege and gross injustice with a calm, almost accepting eye. He raises our hopes that the girl's death will be avenged, and then, as if to say there is no justice, he destroys that hope. Most important of all, he makes Celestine the most concerned, courageous, and nonapathetic of his characters, so that when she fails and falls back into the oppressive side of the class system, we need only Joseph's political victory to complete the cycle of despair. Celestine and Joseph are locked together—she by a hideous fascination with his destructive strength, and he by the pittance of respectability he feels he can gain by their marriage. The paradoxes multiply. The rapist-murderer speaks zealously of the moral rebirth of France. Celestine herself despises her masters, then vengefully punishes her second spouse with the indignities of a servant. As for innocence, it goes the way of the little girl, whose violent death is never avenged. The frustration of ideals and the reversal of values are as complete as any achieved by Bunuel in *Un Chien Andalou,* but they appear in the style of his new surrealism, a calm portrayal of absurdities so complete as to become hallucinatory.

Although religious elements abound in *Diary* they are not central to its subject. This may be why Bunuel returned to the Church, a parallel obsession, in *Simon of the Desert*. This new film also marked a return to Mexico, to the photography of Gabriel Figueroa, and to what has become Bunuel's own repertory company of actors, including the dwarf who played Ujo in *Nazarin*, Sylvia Pinal *(Viridiana* and *Exterminating Angel)*, and Claudio Brook. The subject of *Simon of the Desert* shows Bunuel's capacity, even at the age of sixty-five, to surprise the critics. It is the life of Simon Stylites, the anchorite saint who in the ascetic style of the times passed thirty-seven of his years atop a sixty-foot column near Aleppo, preaching to thousands of pilgrims before his death in the mid-fifth century. The project was a daring one for many reasons, not all of them related to its subject matter. Technically, a film whose action takes place atop a column is not easy to shoot. Furthermore, a film forty-two minutes long requires a companion piece for theatrical release (it was not until Orson Welles' *Immortal Story* was released several years later that *Simon* could be seen, on a double bill, in the United States). Nevertheless, the film received a Special Jury Prize at Venice in 1965.

Simon of the Desert has a light, comic touch that sets it apart as an amusement. Simon, like Nazarin, seems to have appealed to Bunuel if only for his mad devotion to ideals. This may be why the saint is never ridiculed directly in the film. He preaches lofty ideals to the monks and laymen who approach him, he humbly refuses ordination to the priesthood, he restores hands to a man who lost them for thievery, and he overcomes a variety of bizarre and amusing temptations. However, he is just a bit dotty, and there exists in him something of the coldness which we detected in Nazarin and in Viridiana, a denial of the human. Simon refuses to comfort his mother, for example. And looking for something to bless, he deliriously finds a crumb of food between his teeth and absentmindedly makes the sign of the cross over it. After overcoming temptations in which Sylvia Pinal makes diabolical appeals to his pride, sexuality, and even his piety (appearing as a bearded female Christ), Simon is swept away (by jet?) into twentieth-century New York. There he and the devil shoulder their way through a crowded discotheque where young people frenziedly dance the "Radioactive Flesh," which the devil assures him is the latest dance—in fact, "the last dance."

The film evidences a grudging admiration for Simon's obsession, the religious fetish so calmly accepted by the Church and people of his time. However, most of the humor, if not directed at Simon, is created at his expense. He heals, but people remain morally unchanged. He is better than the bishop and the envious monks, but not so good as the simple dwarf or his doting mother, whose unceasing labors provide a counterpoint to his ascetical practices and weird mysticism. He overcomes temptations, but we are not quite sure they were not generated by his famished delirium. The film's pattern of unblinking acceptance of the miraculous, followed by the man's failure to change anything, ultimately condemns Simon to irrelevancy. When he is transported into the future (our own day), he falls into passive apathy, an inability to respond to "the devil's work" as embodied in the rock and roll dancers. The benign tone of the film stems from this change which turns frontal attack into a "cold shoulder."

Luis Bunuel turned from the religion of *Simon of the Desert* to the comedy of manners of *Belle de Jour,* following what has become his pattern of alternative genres. The year 1966 did not provide a favorable climate for comedy, but *Belle de Jour* succeeded in proving that the anarchist's aim was still good by sending shock waves throughout the Western world. The film scrutinized the upper classes (as in *Exterminating Angel*), but this time it was in the person of a woman more frigid than Viridiana—a woman given the symbolic name Severine. Her husband Pierre is a charming, loving spouse patient enough to tolerate her frigidity. Severine's problem surfaces in daydreams, bizarre fantasies in which Pierre has her dragged from a carriage, gagged, whipped, and raped by the coachmen as he watches. Their family friend, the roué Husson, in flirting with Severine one day mentions the address of a brothel patronized by rich sophisticates. Severine visits the brothel and is encouraged by Anais, the young Madame, to work there each afternoon under the name Belle De Jour. Instead of being repulsed by the work, Severine is exhilarated, and even feels closer to Pierre. But a young and violent patron, Marcel, falls in love with her, threatening to tell Pierre if she will not go with him. Severine refuses, and Marcel shoots Pierre and is himself shot to death by the police. Pierre is paralyzed for life, unable to speak, but Severine seems to enjoy caring for him, although it means giving up Mme. Anais and the afternoons. Husson knows the truth, however, and persuades her to let him tell Pierre of her afternoon dalliances. In two contrasting endings, both of which are included in the film, Pierre first sheds a silent tear as he hears the truth in complete immobility, then secondly rises from his wheelchair, as if cured by the truth.

Critics have said, with some justification, that *Belle de Jour* represents Bunuel's complete mastery of the surrealist style. *Belle* is also, in many respects, the most difficult of the director's films. Bunuel has created such ambiguities between fantasy and the real, between dream and actuality, that it is all but impossible to separate these elements. But an effect so carefully planned must be intentional, and so whatever our interpretation of the film may be, it seems clear that Bunuel wishes to remind us that these contrasting realms are really one.

As in previous social satires, the rich are shown enjoying vices that have the added pleasure of privilege. Severine can maintain her anonymity as Belle De Jour, just as the rich patrons who frequent the house of Mme. Anais remain nameless. But the worst indictment of the rich is the psychological perversity which makes it possible for her to enjoy sexual pleasure only in sordid, clandestine surroundings where her reputation is always endangered. Husson finds her out, but once he learns she is corrupt, he no longer desires her (although he does not betray her). She bends the thug, Marcel, to her will, but is unable to keep him from destroying Pierre—if, indeed, that really takes place. Throughout the film, we are never certain whether Severine is dreaming, daydreaming, or actually experiencing what we see. And when the twofold ending portrays Pierre at once killed and cured by the news of her infidelity, we begin to suspect the entire film exists only in Bunuel's festering imagination.

There is, of course, no need to choose, to select what is real and what is unreal, because it is precisely this ambiguity that serves to make the director's point. We see once again how repressed sexuality breeds refined, perverted humanity. As always, however, there is no judgment on persons so afflicted. The unreal quality of *Belle*'s images and action is underscored by the hallucinatory sounds of carriage bells and train whistles, the mysterious appearance of cats, and a color photography full of the beauty of bright, shiny toys and fairytale castles.

It is interesting to note that Bunuel has carried his social satires from the conditions of the poor *(Las Hurdes* and *Los Olvidados)* to the salons of the rich exploiters *(Diary of a Chambermaid* and *Belle de Jour)*. As with Fellini and the neo-realists, his concerns have followed his fortunes (a fact which does not necessarily place Bunuel among the exploiters). Rich and poor alike form Bunuel's private world, one which has not changed much from the salon of *L'Age d'Or* to the brothel of Mme. Anais. But in each film (particularly in *Exterminating Angel*), he has added a new dimension to his indictment. His charges become more and more specific until in *Belle de Jour* the accusations are unbearable.

Bunuel's "religious" films have undergone an evolution similar to that in his social satires and black morality plays. The frontal assualt of *Un Chien Andalou* and

L'Age d'Or mellowed into the personal studies of Nazarin
and Viridiana, while a more schematic presentation is
evident in Simon of the Desert, a man who had supposedly achieved perfection. But suddenly, out of the
popular success of *Belle de Jour,* the director unleashed a
formidable theological critique which so threatened religion at its conceptual foundations that the critics were
helpless. The work that accomplished this remarkable
effect is deceptively called *The Milky Way.*

The continental title for this 1970 film is *St. James'
Way,* referring to the pilgrimage to the shrine of St. James
Compostella in Spain. The "field of stars" (campo-stella)
is a famous place of pilgrimage, and so *The Milky Way* is
a pilgrims' progress, featuring two vagrants of dubious
spirituality as the pilgrims. In reality, the film is a journey
through Church history, a guided tour of the dogmatic
jungles of Catholic theology, with famous heretics as the
guides. It would be difficult to describe this picaresque
journey. There is no chronology, sequence, or dramatic
logic of any kind to bind together the adventures of
Pierre and Jean. And yet the episodes add up to a
surprisingly coherent overview. The world through which
they travel is one in which crucial theological issues are
constantly argued, even fought as duels, by everyone—
that is, everyone but the pilgrims themselves. *Their* theol-
ogizing goes no further than a sophomoric challenge that
God demonstrate his existence by a lightning bolt. Cops
discuss the mode of Christ's presence in the Eucharist,
waiters muse over the hypostatic union, and little school
girls recite a litany of heresies capped by the curse,
"anathema sit." The journey weaves drunkenly back and
forth in time, visiting periods of Jansenist determinism,
listening to words of Priscillian dualism, and even featuring several episodes from the life of Christ. At journey's
end, the pair is turned from their goal by a car-hop
prostitute who tells them the shrine is deserted. Pilgrims
are few and unbelieving, she says, but she is selling . . .

and so they give up the pilgrimage for a frolic in the grass. The last scene features Christ's cure of the two blind men, who follow in his footsteps, to a point.

Jean and Pierre are among the most nondescript of Bunuel's peasant heroes, but they bear the only marks of sanity in a wilderness of theological fools. They are first, foremost, and always interested in such basics as food, lodging, and simple bodily pleasures. Like Simon's mother, like the butler in *Exterminating Angel,* and like the servants in *Viridiana,* they are pragmatic, hardheaded, and somewhat confused by all the theological debate around them. In Bunuel's view they alone are human. The doctrines debated are treated with fastidious accuracy by Bunuel, who did his homework so well that neither Church nor heretic will be able to call foul. But as in the case of Bunuel's acceptance of Simon's sanctity, the whole topheavy structure of conceptual rationalization is tumbled by a shrug and a "so what?" Both Simon and the theological endeavor are irrelevant. The shock is not that the bums should accede to the whore's invitation, but that they should have gone on a pilgrimage at all. If it is true that Bunuel remains the demythologizing genius of his earliest films, then this film is his *chef d'oeuvre,* and thus worthy of the analysis we will devote to it in the pages to come.

Bunuel, as the protagonist of a completely innovative career, has been judged time and again to have no surprises left to give us. He himself, as a matter of fact, has regularly predicted his retirement. But his vision remains incomplete, his obsessions unsatisfied, and so he continues to produce, almost in spite of himself. Critical response seems to indicate that the master of anarchy is repeating himself in his 1971 work *Tristana.*

The mellowness which *Tristana* exudes is as much a function of the autumnal tones of the Toledo locations as it is of the softened accents of Bunuel's social satire. Tristana, the ward of an elderly bon vivant, Don Lope (an extension of Don Jaime in *Viridiana?),* comes to live with him. As a child, she had feared him like the devil (her dreams still portray his severed head as the clapper on a church bell), but his tentative advances easily seduce her. The greying womanizer soon learns, however, that he has taken on a porcelain valkyrie. She runs off with a young artist, leaving Don Lope in poverty and social disgrace. But she returns with a diseased leg that must be amputated, and now "seducing" him in return, she persuades him to marry her. Don Lope rapidly declines in health and self-esteem, while Tristana hops about grotesquely on her one leg, amusing herself by exposing her body to the deaf-mute caretaker. One night she finds Don Lope in the midst of a heart attack, and raising the phone to call the doctor, she instead slowly lowers it in revenge to its cradle.

Tristana is a tale of vengeance, but the avenger may be Bunuel rather than the delicate fury of the title. Don Lope embodies so many faults of the old Spain of Franco that one wonders how the film was made. His destruction is a masterpiece of subtle cruelties, reducing him to the ultimate indignity of sipping chocolate with clerics, an old man who "got religion." There is no coherent motivation for Tristana's actions; her seduction and revenge are elements of a larger destiny of which she is in part the victim. The side streets of Toledo evoke the passivity of Spain, the molten lava crusted over for the time being. The doomed Don Lope is the messenger of a society which has lost its soul—freedom. Bunuel need not, of course, explicitly articulate this thesis. It emerges clearly in the pathetic antics of the old hypocrite, his concerns over money, the vanity of his fading vigor, and his courtly acceptance of the crippled but deadly scorpion Tristana into his household. Adverse critical judgments of Tristana may stem from too-detailed a knowledge of Bunuel's earlier films, and from the deja vu feeling generated by a film that would have derived greater impact had it stood alone. There is also an interesting possibility that Bunuel is showing the last stages of his own evolution in the pathetic image of Don Lope sipping chocolate in the rectory. Bunuel was seventy when he made the film, and like Don Lope he cannot hope to die at the barricades.

Nevertheless, Bunuel continues to enrich an already productive career with works that·extend his vision into new areas of concern. His latest film at this writing is, if anything, more youthful than most of his productions, not only because of its lightly comic satirical thrust, but also for its unwonted topicality. Its title, *The Discreet Charm of the Bourgeoisie,* marks it as a return to the concerns of *The Exterminating Angel,* but its tone is less savage and didactic. Critics have even detected a trace of reluctant admiration for his lifetime foes in the tolerance with which Bunuel re-catalogs their vices.

In spite of many familiar elements, the film manages to incorporate more references to the world at large than any other of his social satires. The absence of such topics has been paradoxical in Bunuel. The great events of contemporary history through which Bunuel lived—World Wars I and II, the Cold War, the reconstruction of Europe, and the Western world's counterculture revolutions—can be sought for in vain in the body of his films. There are, of course, exceptions such as the cameo reference to Rock culture in the last scene of *Simon of the Desert,* where young people on a crowded dance floor gyrate to "The Radioactive Flesh." More typically, *Viridiana,* *Nazarin* and *Tristana* take place in a timeless universe that resembles no historical setting in particular. It is the world of *Belle de Jour,* and of *The Milky Way,* a world so void of identifying characteristics that its drama seems part of a relentless, eternal struggle by which the details of evil's triumph over good are worked out. When we recall this Bunuellian world, we are shocked to note how precisely *The Discreet Charm of the Bourgeoisie* is set in the present. War and revolution make their presence known, the topic of heroin smuggling is central to the action, and the film even makes an oblique reference to Church reform.

The Discreet Charm of the Bourgeoisie may become the parting salvo in a war that began with Bunuel's silent classics and developed in The Exterminating Angel—the war on the bourgeoisie. Ten years after this savage attack, the director reverses the plot to play new variations on its savage absurdities. Unlike the stranded rich of Rue de la Providence, who cannot leave the meal, the bourgeoisie of the more recent film find it impossible to fulfill their eternally postponed dinner engagement. Fernando Rey, ambassador of the fictitious South American country Miranda, masterminds a top-level Paris heroin ring exporting to the lucrative U.S. drug market. His "business associates" are two chic Parisian couples, the young Senechals and the more mature Thevenots, plus Mme. Thevenot's sister. They plan an elaborate dinner to celebrate a drug-smuggling coup that has netted them a fortune, and the comedy of the film consists in the endless frustrations of this design.

The four arrive at the Senechal's country home, but nothing is prepared. . . . they are a day early, and M. Senechal is out of town. They resolve to make the best of it and take Mme. Senechal to dinner, but they find it impossible to eat—the restaurant owner has died, and his body is laid out in one of the dining rooms. The women try to have lunch, but a soldier interrupts with his sad tale of how his mother's ghost persuaded him to poison his father. Another attempt to lunch at the Senechals is sidetracked by a fit of amorous passion (amour fou) that sends the hosts out a window to couple on the lawn, while the hungry guests wait patiently. Phone calls, doorbells, and uninvited guests add to the list of interruptions. At one point the meal seems well under way when a detachment of soldiers on maneuvers politely intrude. They gauchely accept a perfunctory invitation to stay, but the meal is stopped again by a young soldier's narrative concerning the bloody murder of a police sergeant. Finally, the roast lamb is on the table, the plates are full, the wine poured, when the police break into the room to arrest the bourgeois celebrants for smuggling drugs.

Not quite a comedy of manners, *The Discreet Charm of the Bourgeoisie* nevertheless· evokes recollections of Oscar Wilde, and of Restoration Comedy drawing room farces. It is the unbelievable imperturbability of the protagonists, their supreme self-possession in the midst of social and political disaster, that gives the film its satirical comic thrust. There is a kind of mad inventiveness enabling them to find a way out of any crisis. Their journey through life is crystallized in a recurring shot of the six sophisticates, striding in twos and threes down some country road, on their way to a meal that never takes place. Nor is it the meal alone that remains unconsummated. The friends, as we have noted, interrupt the amorous embraces of the Senechals. And the inept ambassador's afternoon affair with Mme. Thevenot suffers the unexpected arrival of her husband, who is too polite to do more than ask quietly what his friend was doing there at midday. Casual remarks, earnest inquiries, involved conversations are never completed in this world of bourgeois charm.

Although Bunuel does not rip the veneer of respectability from them, as in the claustrophobic confinement of *The Exterminating Angel,* he does show the price paid for their foolish pleasures, their vintage wines, table delicacies, and sophisticated prattle. Fernando Rey, in an extension of his role in *The French Connection,* poisons lives by heroin in order to indulge his tastes for the perfect martini or the best cut of lamb. When police demand to search his diplomatic pouch he is genuinely outraged, convincing in the belief of his own immunity. In fact, this immunity is at the core of Bunuel's case against the bourgeoisie. They go through life with a passport bearing an invisible stamp, exempting them from most of life's suffering, and all of its moral obligations.

Their dreamlike lives, the waking fantasy in which they spend their days, is often comically invaded by reality: soldiers on maneuver, the local bishop offering his services as gardener, a haunted young man who has poisoned his father, and finally police who have cracked the heroin ring. But none of these invasions jar them off course, so that their lives proceed with the self-contained luxury of a cruise ship, an eternal vacation subsidized by slave-like workers one almost never sees.

Bunuel seems to say that the bourgeoisie can take frustrations with equanimity because they know life has never denied them anything for long. Before heroin other forms of business existed, and before that, colonialism and slavery. For the future, one must have confidence, both in one's class, and in its single most precious talent—survival. They are a ridiculous lot: the girl who passes out on one martini, the ambassador who muffs an afternoon affair, the couple who make love on the lawn. Like so many of Bunuel's characters, they are on the way *(Mexican Bus Ride, Nazarin, The Milky Way)*, but have no idea where they are going. Prisoners of a life constricted of social amenities, they are content because they designed the prison they live in. And Bunuel, even as he snaps at their heels, seems to admire their inflappable style, which he euphemistically refers to as their "discreet charm." In the desperate hour of the police raid, the ambassador could have remained hidden under the table, but he betrays himself by reaching for that last, perfectly done slide of roast lamb. How can the outraged anarchist hate an enemy capable of such a gesture?

When Luis Bunuel announced he was accepting the Franco government's offer to shoot *Viridiana* in Spain, even his loyal supporters shouted betrayal. But when the picture appeared, they had to eat their harsh judgments. They should have known better than to doubt him. Beginning with his iconoclastic surrealist films, and going on through a long period of commercial failures and successes, the director always remained true to his "moral

code," his contempt for "conventional morality, traditional sacred cows, sentimentality and all that moral filth
of society which comes into it." Then, beginning with
Los Olvidados (and now superbly equipped for his task),
he began the series of social satires and religious melo-
dramas in which he worked out his private vision. We
have called this process the "evolution of an anarchist,"
but the development has been too orderly for anarchy.
The development we have described has cast Bunuel in
the role of official blasphemer, negator of myths, and
chief cinematic herald of the Death of God. But before
we accept these appellations, we had best take an overview of Bunuel's chaotic cosmos, his profound musings
on the mystery of iniquity, and his constant reproach to
the Christian to produce some evidence of the continued
presence of a good God in a world of evil.

3

The Chaotic Cosmos:
Bunuel's Private World

The capsule descriptions which constitute the preceding survey of Bunuel's development contribute very little to an understanding of his private world. As useful as they may be for readers who have not seen his films, these brief analyses only encircle with words his emotional and conceptual milieu. Bunuel's is a world of images and sounds, of beautifully photographed reality evoking elusive resonances, of cryptic dialogue burdened with double entendres. And, with intentional paradox, it is a "chaotic cosmos," for it replaces all the orderly structure we associate with the cosmos, substituting his own views of good and evil, innocence and guilt, religion and atheism. For this reason, descriptions of his "stories" may be the worst possible index to his thematic preoccupations.

Nevertheless, Bunuel's images and symbols, his surreal effects and metaphysical jokes are hung, as it were, on a sequence of scenes which at least help to define them. The plot details of *Los Olvidados* and of *Diary of a Chambermaid*, for example, must be known before we can see Pedro and Jaibo, Celestine and Joseph in their interlocking destinies, so characteristic of Bunuel's conception of good and evil. The innocence of Rita *(Viridiana)*, Ochitos *(Los Olvidados)*, and Severine *(Belle*

de Jour) must be established in a personal context before
the significance of their corruption can emerge. And the
horde of blind men, deaf-mutes, those crippled and diseased, those deformed and defective who form a melan-
choly procession through his films must be accounted for
on the surfaces of his personal world before they can be
demonstrated to be part of his view of humanity. Therefore, with full recognition that description and synthesis
can in no way re-create the essence of this Bunuellian
universe, we must now consider the visual, verbal, and
dramatic themes which converge on that mysterious center. They, in turn, may provide a key to his vocation—
demythologizer for a post-Christian age.

The Mystery of Iniquity

Bunuel is a man hypnotically fascinated with evil, yet
bent on proving it doesn't exist. There is, for example, a
level of meaning under all his symbols, fetishes, characters, and plots which takes sides in a cosmic struggle
between good and evil. He didn't create the struggle, and
at times seems to long for a ceasefire, but he returns
compulsively to what tradition, culture, and especially
religion call "evil." Even though he does not use the
term, he may be trying to tell us something of the moral
schizophrenia of our Manichean lives.

Bunuel's films jolt a viewer indulged by the mass media
with visions of unblemished physical beauty, because
they are filled with the outcasts of society, the blind, the
deaf, the diseased, the mutilated. The symbolic meaning
of blindness was made clear already in the opening scene
of *Un Chien Andalou.* The vicious blind beggar of *Los
Olvidados* is terrorized by young toughs, but he is just as
cruel as they. He has a tongue as deadly as his nail-
studded club, and he is not above collecting a few pesetas
for giving quack medical advice. He molests little girls.
The blind man to whom Nazarin gives alms gives him an

unctuous blessing, but when he is refused, he curses and reviles his benefactor. In *L'Age d'Or*, the frustrated Modot angrily kicks a blind man in one of his rages. And we are soon aware that of all the vagabonds Viridiana has taken into her community the most vicious and lecherous of all is the blind Don Amalio, who takes the central place of Christ in the parody of the Last Supper.

The young boy whom Tristana tantalizes by exposing herself is a deaf-mute locked in a hopeless desire for one he can never possess. Tristana herself is one of many lame characters, her wooden leg providing some scenes of macabre humor. Among Viridiana's wards are the lame, and Jaibo's street gang in *Los Olvidados* amuse themselves by tipping a legless man from his cart and watching him roll helplessly in the gutter as the car is sent careening down the street. The pattern that emerges from these episodes and scenes is physical evil compounded by human cruelty and indifference. The thief whose amputated hands are restored by Simon of the Desert gives no thanks; the witnessing crowd only murmurs the casual admiration, "not bad!" In *Subida al Cielo* a man's wooden leg gets stuck in a riverbed. And finally, Belle's husband ends up (whether in reality or fantasy) in a wheelchair, paralyzed completely except for his ability to shed tears.

These deformed individuals do not generate pity, and if we were inclined to sympathize with them, their viciousness, stupidity, or greed would dissuade us. But they are part of the frieze of ills that border Bunuel's people environment. The resentment of these unfortunates is repulsive. The beggar with the diseased arm in *Viridiana* delights in dipping it in holy water founts so the pious will share his infection. Furthermore, we are given the impression that human deformity and such unnecessary ills as malnutrition are the norm. In his later films, such as *The Discreet Charm of the Bourgeoisie*, Bunuel deals with the upper class who are already insulated from suffering; the militia of mutilated, therefore, appears less frequently. There is, however, a recurrent figure treated most sympathetically by Bunuel—the dwarf Ujo, from *Nazarin*, whose touching devotion to the prostitute Andara puts the cold-hearted priest to shame.

For Bunuel, human physical deformity is not the totality of the world's evil, but simply part of a universe badly made. The barren rocks on the shore of *Un Chien Andalou* and *L'Age d'Or* are his view of the world. In *Los Olvidados*, the skyscrapers of Mexico City are just visible across the rubble of demolished buildings that borders the slums. Civilization seems hardly to have touched the isolated town of *Las Hurdes*, a barren heap of rock without water, without soil, almost without life. Simon of the Desert looks out from his perch across a ruthless wasteland with whirlpools of dust stirred by the wind. True, in later films Bunuel permits more background beauty, such as the streets of Toledo in *Tristana*, but most often the beauty appears in contrast to moral degradation, as in the case of *Belle de Jour*, and in the comfortable affluence of the "beautiful people" in *The Discreet Charm of the Bourgeoisie*. Aside from these recent respites, there is only the jungle of *La Mort en ce Jardin*, the desert island of *Robinson Crusoe* (with its cruel mirages), or the invading greenery imperiling the bus in *Subida al Cielo*.

But for Bunuel the mystery of iniquity is most evident in man, where it appears not in St. Paul's paradox of choosing the evil one does not will, but rather in our lack of freedom to choose. There is a fate which frustrates human aspirations, a fate identical with the Bunuellian irony. Persons become agents of unknown forces, like the trapped aristocrats of *The Exterminating Angel;* the more idealistic they are *(Nazarin* and *Viridiana)* the more cruelly they are frustrated. In *Los Olvidados* everyone who tries to better his condition is killed violently. Traditionally, these reversals would be seen as the triumph of evil over good. But Bunuel seems to challenge the very premise of a Good and an Evil universe, of a personal antagonism between a good God and an evil Devil in which he sees man as the loser. If he appears to overbalance one side of our own dichotomy, it may be that he is not taking sides, but attempting to blur permanently in our sensibilities the one-sided distinction itself.

The chaos of Bunuel's private world emerges most forcefully in the microcosm of man. Here we begin to see a reason for his obsessive visual motifs and, possibly, for his thematic preoccupations. Bunuel does not substitute a naive humanism for the religion he attacks and rejects. His men, major and secondary characters alike, are defective. Although he has told an interviewer, "I love all men," we must interpret this profession in terms of the image of man in Bunuel's films. Man, as we have seen, is often diseased, deformed, and deprived. Even those relatively whole are seen in terms of what the culture considers the least noble aspects of man. Here Bunuel's obsession with feet becomes significant. He is like the genteel Don Jaime of *Viridiana,* who lovingly dwells on the feet of Rita as she skips rope. The old grandfather of *Diary of a Chambermaid,* who is Don Jaime's counterpart, is a foot fetishist who died clutching the ladies' boots from which he derived such pathetic consolations. Feet are often an object of passion *(L'Age d'Or),* of sensuality (as Pedro's mother bathes her feet, in *Los Olvidados*), of sadistic religiosity (in the ceremony of footwashing in *El*), or of sexual indifference (*El Bruto* carefully removes his shoes and socks before he makes love). In the most evident episode, the lovers of *L'Age d'Or* seem obsessed by feet: Modot is distracted by the feet of the male statue, and after he is called away Lya Lys is found sucking the toe of the same statue. Feet, then, are a constant reminder of our frail humanity, embodying all the vulnerability of the "Achilles heel," or "feet of clay."

A similar observation might be made about hair in Bunuel's films. The girl caught by her hair in the jungle underbrush of *La Mort en ce Jardin* is a deaf-mute, and this relationship between hair and speech is a carry-over from *Un Chien Andalou,* where the cyclist torments the girl with a grotesque "beard" of hair apparently taken from her own armpit. Like our feet, which touch the earth and remind us we are not angels, hair has long been featured in myth and legend. Hair adds to this human frailty the connotations of the onset of puberty. For the repressed it will always evoke the panic that physiological change precipitates. This may be why in the last scene of *L'Age d'Or* Bunuel goes from the marcelled hair of De Blangis as the holy-picture Jesus to a cross planted in the snow with pubic hair marking the place of the wounds.

This man is still an animal, Bunuel says, earthbound with feet of clay and a body partly covered with hair. He is flesh, and an eater of flesh like other carnivores. This may explain the frequency of slaughterhouse settings in *El Bruto* and also in *La Illusion Viaja en Tranvia,* where workers on a free bus ride hang their sides of beef from the luggage racks. The last indignity to which the mesmerized aristocrats of *Exterminating Angel* are subjected is to be forced to slaughter their own meat, the sheep once intended for their entertainment, but now essential to their survival. Perhaps the most frightening reminder of fleshly mortality comes in Pedro's dream in *Los Olvidados.* When he expresses his frustrated love, his mother answers his cry for affection with frighteningly erotic abandon, but then when he accuses her of refusing him food, she turns in hideous slow motion and offers him a repellent, shapeless slab of meat.

We are flesh, Bunuel says again and again, and so we are not much different from the meat we eat or the animals from which it comes. These animals roam through Bunuel's films like the bear in *Exterminating Angel,* a disturbingly concrete form of man's passions unleashed. The barking dogs of *Viridiana,* like the mysterious "bull" of which Rita speaks, are heralds of evil and passion. The slinking alley dog of *Los Olvidados* is Jaibo's alter ego. The animal is often the inhabitant of man's own psyche, a repressed desire looking for escape. The putrescent donkeys of *Un Chien Andalou* are straight out of the cyclist's subconscious, and they reappear in *Las Hurdes* as beasts of burden who have plunged over the cliff and are now infested with the bees they were carrying. Insects can be altogether fearsome in Bunuel's films, where they receive an ex-entomologist's expert attention. They seem to represent irrational fears (the death's head moth of *Un Chien Andalou*), dreaded for their sting (the scorpions of *L'Age d'Or*), and occasionally the objects of a tender but futile human attention (the drowning bee rescued by Uncle Jaime, in *Viridiana*). The cats of *Belle de Jour*'s fantasies, as well as the bulls named Expiation and Remorse, add new dimensions to Bunuel's bestiary of analogies to the human condition.

As he explores human vulnerability, Bunuel uncovers sexuality as a central factor, and he does so in a way that shocks many audiences. But sex is a feature much misunderstood in his films, often receiving very superficial analysis by critics. For Bunuel, sexuality appears to be a disease that most humans never outlive, a malady already terminal at puberty, something to be tolerated quietly until it is ended by death. The relative absence of normal or joyful sexuality has given the director's films a name for perversion. The first impression of sexuality in Bunuel's films is one of confusion, for Bunuel seems bent on blurring sexual polarities as much as he is intent on demolishing good/evil dichotomies. Long before the "unisex revolution," Bunuel was obscuring sexual differences by introducing ambiguities, as in the reversal of sexual mores apparent in the effeminate cyclist and masculine woman on the street in *Un Chien Andalou*. He first presented his thesis that sexual perversity results from moralistic repression of natural impulses in *L'Age d'Or*. The lovers pitifully grapple from their wicker chairs and are endlessly interrupted in their Tristan-accompanied love idyll. Western culture has sublimated sexuality by relating it to death, an evil mating often represented in

Bunuel's images. Sleepwalking Viridiana scatters ashes on
the frustrated nuptial bed of Don Jaime, and the doomed
lovers of *Exterminating Angel* exclaim "My Love! My
Death!" after the body of Russell is stuffed into the
hiding place for their suicidal mating. According to
Bunuel, religion is responsible for this sick sexuality of
death. Nazarin coolly fondles a snail as the women jeal-
ously puzzle out their love for him, telling them of a
"universal love" that will never satisfy their passion.

Other images of repression abound. The jealous monster of *El Bruto* is an acolyte for a feet-washing ceremony
in church when he first sees the shapely legs of the
woman he will hound to death. The Church has kept him
celibate past forty, and when he is free to act, his pent-up
passion takes perverse forms. Fowls are often intercut to
emphasize human passions, in the tradition of the lecherous cock of the legend. Like a weathercock, these feath-
ered friends tell the direction of human life according to
the shifting winds of passion. The sexual bestiary multi-
plies almost to absurdity: a cat pounces on a mouse as
Don Jorge amusedly complies with Ramona's passion in
Viridiana; a boar routs a rabbit as the lecherous Joseph of
Diary of a Chambermaid attacks the little girl. The giant
black bull "seen" by Rita after she witnesses Don Jaime
attempting to rape the drugged Viridiana is a familiar
motif. Like the bulls named Expiation and Remorse in
Belle de Jour, the animal of sexuality is related to guilt
and punishment. Sexuality may be the least developed
dimension of our humanity, Bunuel seems to say, and so
long as it continues to be denied, he will remind us of it
at every turn.

The Perils of Innocence

Bunuel's chaotic cosmos seems most overburdened
with "evil" when it ruthlessly destroys the two safeguards
of the good—innocence and religion. The most common
image of innocence in his films is the not-quite-innocent

child. Rita, in *Viridiana*, is altogether too precocious: she
skips rope with the suicide weapon, senses the "bulls" of
passionate evil abroad, and burns the ex-novice's crown
of thorns. The street children of *Los Olvidados* are anything but innocent when they turn over the amputee's
cart, and the one who *is* innocent is quickly corrupted by
Jaibo. Bunuel never forgot the town in *Las Hurdes*, where
children were deprived of bread because parents did not
know what it was. Even when innocence appears to
conquer, it is merely victimized. The little girl in *Subida
al Cielo* who led by a string the pair of oxen towing the
bus out of the mud is shortly thereafter carried in a
coffin by that same bus. Her death resembles that of the
Hurdanos child, bitten by a scorpion, her body consigned
to the river. No less arbitrary is the death of the Mongoloid boy in *L'Age d'Or*, shot by his gamekeeper father
for interfering with his smoking. Innocence is a survival
hazard.

There is something faintly sinister in childhood innocence—perhaps a foretaste of the excesses of maturity.
The school girls in *Milky Way* chant with clear, young
voices the litany of heresies which ends with the refrain,
"Let him be cursed!" Archibaldo de la Cruz was similarly
corrupted in his youth by the lie that his music box had
the power to execute his destructive wishes. A metaphor
for a childhood never allowed expression is the deaf-mute
of *Tristana*, confidante of Don Lope and secret admirer
of the perverse heroine. Adult innocence, after all, is no
more effective than childhood innocence. *Nazarin's* hero
is "innocent" of the ways of the world, but it makes him
coldly insensitive to the needs and desires of his disciples,
Beatriz and Andara. Viridiana is equally innocent of
sexuality, more a child than Rita, who is precocious in
evil. The novice shudders when offered the cow's udder
for milking; she prefers to express her sexuality symbolically in her sleepwalking episodes. Perhaps the most
"innocent" of all is Simon of the Desert, simple-minded
enough to mistake Sylvia Pinal for the Good Shepherd.

Even the chaste, faithful Belle De Jour turns to genteel afternoon prostitution as if she were returning to a long deferred vocation. And, of course, she likes it.

Bunuel's favorite shock tactic is to destroy innocence, but he does so in order to prove his point that it constitutes no protection and is likely to cause great harm. Nazarin once liberated creates trouble wherever he goes. The victims of his innocence are not only his faithful women, but the railroad gang that rejects him (where he indirectly causes a shooting), in the plague town (where his services threaten to separate lovers at the moment of death), and even in prison (where he sets the "good thief" against the "bad thief"). Whether the innocence is ignorance of one's own animal nature (smells, desires, hair, feet) or a negative state of original goodness, it fails to overcome evil. The dramatic plots of Bunuel's films are classic reversals of this kind. In *Diary of a Chambermaid*, the innocent child raped and murdered is not avenged, and all of Celestine's work (and self-compromise) to reveal Joseph's guilt comes to naught. Viridiana's innocence of the basic corruption of her vagrant charges fosters her illusion that the monastic regimen will transform them into good Christians. The orgy and attempted rape are the results of her naive trust. Even Nazarin's life of service collapses when the offer of a pineapple becomes a trauma for one who never learned to receive as well as to give.

The traditional triumph of good over evil is so completely reversed in Bunuel's works that exceptions are extremely rare. The pattern of hopes dashed and optimism frustrated that is established in *Las Hurdes* persists throughout his career. No one avenges, or even mourns, Pedro's death in *Los Olvidados;* in fact, the camera hardly notes his passing. Far from completing their pilgrimage, the vagrants in *The Milky Way* romp with a whore while their goal is in sight. Even Robinson Crusoe crumbles under the desert island wilderness he attempted to civilize, and the jealous fool of *El Bruto* deteriorates from a devout acolyte to attempted murderer of a priest. In *Tristana*, we watch horrified as the demure porcelain girl (Catherine Deneuve is the ideal image of innocence) first accedes to Don Lope's nervous passion, then disfigured turns upon him to fulfill her dreams of his head serving as clapper for the church bell. Each film ends with an image frustrating our expectations of the victory of good over evil: Nazarin dazedly accepting the piece of fruit whose significance he dare not question; Viridiana abstractedly playing cards with cousin Jorge and his mistress Ramona; the aristocrats of *Exterminating Angel* in the church, captive once more to their superstitions; Simon of the Desert helpless in a modern world no longer convinced of sin and temptation; the vagrant pilgrims of *The Milky Way* ending their "spiritual" journey carnally; and Don Lope, bent over his cup of chocolate, mouthing pious platitudes in the company of clerics. The victory may seem complete, but one foe has not yet been destroyed—religion.

Where Is Your God?

The perils of innocence, the triumph of evil over good, and the very confusion of the combat between these forces make Bunuel's work a cinematic "Devil's Dictionary." Bunuel protests that he loves man, but he paints him deformed, vulnerable in his innocence, a stranger to his bodily needs, and the victim of his violent, perverted sexuality. The wasteland of Bunuel's moral universe, where the battle haze of the good/evil struggle has obliterated all boundaries, is also the burial ground of organized religion. Bunuel continues to cry out to his tormented characters, in effect, "Where *is* your God?" He is like his Robinson Crusoe, hysterically shouting the words of the Psalms but receiving only a mocking, perverse echo. The mystery of iniquity which he has explored throughout a lifetime is nothing more than the good/evil conflict he was taught as a child, but which he stopped believing long ago. His attack focuses on the battle itself, and his prime target is the source of the siege mentality—the Church, its officials, its rituals and symbols, its sheeplike devoted ones, its saints and ascetics, and its myths of promised immortality.

For some, this spells anticlericalism. But this is too facile a category for so complex a foe of institutional Christianity as Bunuel. It is far more enlightening to present his portrait of the Church in the context of his larger vision, where the battle between good and evil appears as a futile war and a false dichotomy. For Bunuel, the Church has created the false issue in order to profit from the atmosphere of fear by ruling through guilt and repression. Pretending power over the world of "good and evil" is hypocritical. Church service is either irrelevant or positively harmful to man. The hierarchy, in Bunuel's conception, is the cluster of mitred skeletons stranded on the barren rocks in *L'Age d'Or*. The reverence shown them by the Majorcans indicates that Church power has grown to embrace a whole "new Rome," an establishment of the rich, cultured, and aristocratic. The same image applies to the clergy and the religious throughout Bunuel's films—their plump, faintly effeminate faces expressing a mixture of professional concern and bizarre innocence. Outside of Nazarin himself, the priests are comfortable, self-centered men of the world. One of them employs Nazarin to roll cigarettes for him. The old clerics with whom the aging Don Lope consorts at the end of *Tristana* are of the same fraternity. The bishop who insists upon ordaining Simon adds to the portrait a touch of arrogance, and a wistful admiration for the anchorite. Earlier views of the clergy associated them with active repression of sexuality, like the two clerics in *Un Chien Andalou* who find themselves among the incredible debris of psychic paraphernalia the cyclist must tow along on his way to the object of his passion. Later films treat the clergy gently as part of a background of the establishment.

Nazarin heads the list of Bunuel's indictments of the clergy. What makes the film so important is that most would agree Nazarin is a good priest. He is actively living and suffering the counsels of Christ by living among and serving the poor, a life style for which he is persecuted. But Nazarin unhappily makes things worse. He lectures Andara on solid doctrine as she is recovering from her wounds, but she rewards him by burning what remains of his possessions when she leaves. He tells Beatriz of "universal love," but she is unconsciously attracted to him as a man. When the railroad crew challenges him for working below their wage scale, Nazarin meekly leaves, but he leaves violence behind him. He defends the poor by upbraiding a bullying officer who demands that a passing peasant defer to a priest. The officer is going to shoot Nazarin, but the priest suggests that he must be one of those preachers from the north, that is, a Protestant, since no *priest* would challenge the socio-religious system. And in his attempt to comfort the woman dying of plague, Nazarin tries to tell her of heaven when all she can think of is her lover, Juan. The mayor of the plague town has all the help he needs—Nazarin and his "community" can move on. Meekness does not save Nazarin or convert the evil bandit with whom he is imprisoned and who persecutes him. Even the kindly thief who takes his side admits he does not believe, and then gently takes Nazarin's money "for safe keeping." Nazarin's prayers over the dying child become the occasion for superstitious awe when the child recovers. In each episode, Nazarin is "right," his actions and motives are "good," but the result is harm to those he serves and to himself. A benign interpretation of this action would take it as evidence that Christ, were he to come again, would (as Bunuel himself has suggested) be crucified again. But it seems to me that Bunuel is making another point. Christ need not come again, either in his own person or as another man (Nazarin) because man does not need him.

Another Christian who tries to lead a good life—

Viridiana—is similarly defeated, her work either irrelevant or harmful. Nuns had appeared in *L'Age d'Or*, protectively accompanying Lya Lys after she had been torn from her lover. Viridiana, however, is actually only a novice on the eve of final vows. Nevertheless she is committed to the convent, and when the Mother Superior suggests that she visit her benefactor, Uncle Jaime, she resists the idea. Later, after her uncle's suicide, Viridiana appears in a more favorable light when she encounters her superior and refuses to return. The superior accuses her of pride in remaining outside the convent, and her icy "forgiveness" after their contretemps is hypocritical. Viridiana's determination to live as a Christian, however, takes the form of organizing her beggars, separating them by sex, determining their lives for them, and paternalistically caring for all their needs. They pray at regular intervals, although their hearts are not in it; and one is encouraged to paint a religious painting. In effect, Viridiana becomes the "mother superior," structuring Christian life according to the only form she knows, a highly institutionalized one. Ultimately she is so coldly insensitive to the needs of her charges that they turn on her. They call her an angel of mercy, but she has a coldness which Bunuel traces to her mysticism, more ascetical than contemplative. In her nightwalking sequence, Viridiana acts out her unconscious repressions, scattering ashes over her Uncle's bed. At other times she is busy with her devotions (the objects of torture that remind her of Christ's passion) and her penances (sleeping on rough boards, wearing coarse clothing, hiding her long, blonde hair). She is fearful of her senses (Jorge's cigar nauseates her) and especially of touch (the cow's udder traumatizes her). A grim portrait.

Viridiana fails her beggars, and their orgy is a secret retaliation. Hers is a kind of innocence that destroys, since her trust of the patently untrustworthy sentences them to failure. She has no idea of the vicious bickering, jealousies, and sexual hanky-panky that her holy poor still enjoy in their semi-monastic community. All of this comes out in the "last supper" orgy where they feast, drink, make love, and destroy what they touch, including Viridiana. Her cousin Jorge, who had scoffed at her practices from a distance, is the practical one, saving her from rape by violence—encouraging one beggar to kill the other for money. And at the end of the film she appears to capitulate to Jorge's worldly-wise, amoral pragmatism, coming to "play cards" with him and his servant/mistress. Like Nazarin, she is not the "ordinary" nun, dominating children in schools stronger in discipline than education. But Viridiana's superiority and "innocence" make her unaware of the harm she unleashes in the name of serving mankind. The charge Bunuel levels at her ultimately finds its target in the Church which she represents.

Priest and nun having been demolished, Bunuel turns to *Simon of the Desert* and destroys asceticism. Never does the director question or fault the practices of the anchorite. In fact, his miracles are accepted as authentic, and even his temptations contribute to his otherworldliness. But Simon is less than human. The dwarf, tapping his head, tells him "I don't think you're quite right up here." The evidence is damning. Simon rudely dismisses his mother, who nevertheless builds a hut nearby and cares for herself. His attitudes toward his body are a classical form of asceticism when he counsels the young monk to favor bodily filthiness and disorder as more holy than cleanliness.

Simon is a great example to all Christians, but he requires the service of others who bring him his food and who risk their lives on a rickety ladder to bring him the Eucharist. He overcomes temptations of the flesh (Sylvia Pinal as a sexy young girl in a sailor suit), and of pride (she also appears as the Good Shepherd to tell him his penances are excessive). But gradually one questions his life style, a constant reverie of Latin prayers and inner musings which turn to trivia: "What can I bless now? Blessing is not only a saintly exercise, but it's amusing and hurts no one." The same is true, Bunuel implies, of

Simon's ascetical life. His temptations may or may not be real, but as the monk who visits him observes, "Your penance, like your abstinence, is admirable . . . but of little value to man." Bunuel is not here advocating the active apostolate over the contemplative life, an endeavor that failed in *Viridiana* and *Nazarin*. He is merely noting that none of it serves man, whatever satisfaction it may give to nun, priest, or ascetic. At the end of the film, Simon encounters man in his greatest need, youths dancing "The Radioactive Flesh," a sensual frenzy brought on by the imminence of nuclear holocaust. But he has nothing to say about the evil, in the face of which he is impotent.

Bunuel's critics among the religious institutions have long protested that he takes exaggerated instances, draws caricatures of church figures, and jousts with doctrines and practices long considered obsolete by believers. *The Milky Way* was his answer to his critics. While it is true that he does not abandon his somewhat stereotyped presentation of religion, he fights the Church on its own ground of theology, a point of particular vulnerability. At first it may seem that this film, a guided tour of the most notorious heresies in Church history, amounts to an advocacy of these heresies. Its purposes, however, soon prove to be quite different. As in the case of the religious figures just studied, Bunuel seems less interested in refuting their lives than in proving them irrelevant. In *Milky Way* Bunuel achieves a new level of surrealism by placing abstruse theological debates in the situations of everyday life. The patent absurdity of such casual discussions proves his point. A headwaiter discourses on the two natures of Christ in the hypostatic union; a Spanish padre lectures a young couple (through a locked door!) on the privileges of the Blessed Virgin; a Jesuit furiously duels with a Jansenist as they argue Preventive and Sufficient Grace. Throughout these theological encounters, the two pilgrims remain blandly uninvolved, their concern centering on getting enough to eat, a place to sleep, and the freedom to move on. They seem to represent sanity, common sense, the practical as opposed to the speculative reason. They use bodily and emotional logic in substitution for the film's climate of religious rationalization.

The Church, according to Bunuel, expends its intellectual energies in an elaborate, self-justifying rationalization that only peripherally touches human lives. This is not only absurd, but is a form of insanity. A priest who argues the Patelier heresy on the Eucharist with extreme logic proves to be an escapee from a lunatic asylum. Meanwhile, the vagrants are refused a meal at the inn. Men go hungry while theologians argue on the Bread of Life. A school exercise on the lawn grotesquely develops into a memorized litany of heresies, with hundreds of little girls repeating the refrain, "Let him be cursed!" Excursions into history are equally bizarre. The reinstatement of the heretic Priscillian shows him advising his followers that since the body is evil and restrains the soul, absolute promiscuity is the wisest course. This affirmation of basic human needs is repeated by the two pilgrims who journey to Compostella strangely unconcerned with doctrinal matters. They merely shrug when a nun, in fanatic zeal, has herself nailed to a cross. The film occasionally cuts to a scene from Christ's life where Jesus is presented, not depraved like the Duke de Blangis of *L'Age d'Or*, but rather as a cocky, precipitous young man, admired at a distance by his disciples and a doting "Jewish mother." Jesus' parables are dinner-table anecdotes, delivered for the amusement of his drinking-companion disciples. Within this elaborate, self-justifying structure of the established Church, even the custodians, says Bunuel, do not believe. A priest tells a pious tale of a nun who leaves the convent and returns after many years to find that she was not even missed—the Virgin Mary had taken her place, knowing she would return some day. But as the crowd is nodding appreciation of his story, two men rush in to tell him of a real "miracle" they (and we) have witnessed. The priest does not believe them.

Bunuel does not believe either, but he is willing to concede religion everything it claims except its ability to really serve men. Like the ministry of Nazarin, the good works of Viridiana, and the asceticism of Simon, the theology of *The Milky Way* is simply irrelevant.

The bishop in *The Discreet Charm of the Bourgeoisie* embodies Bunuel's most recent portrait of the hierarchy. The bishop approaches the wealthy Senechals, oblivious of the fact that their wealth comes from heroin smuggling. When they react with surprise to his request for employment as a gardener, he soberly reminds them there can be worker-bishops as well as worker-priests. For Bunuel, this delicious joke has two barbs: do bishops really work?; and in any case, it was the bishops of Rome who stopped the priest-worker movement in postwar France. But the humor cuts deeper. The worker-bishop does well as a gardener, but his new life of "work" does no more good than his life as a bishop. He is, after all, of the same class as the exploiting bourgeoisie for whom he works. They invite him to all their social functions, where his talent for trivia matches theirs. Only at one point does he become human—when he describes how his parents were murdered. But this revelation only sets up the drama of a later scene in which, after hearing the confession identifying a man as his parents' murderer, he gives absolution and then brutally kills him. So much, in Bunuel's view of the hierarchy, for mercy and forgiveness, which are symbolic formalities leaving the inner man unaffected.

Bunuel asks Christians, "Where is your God?" and it is up to them to answer. The Marquis de Sade delivers a lecture on the nonexistence of God, but his victim—a bleeding young girl—zealously confirms that God *is,* so De Sade turns back to his torture. God isn't going to stop him, is he? Human suffering is ultimately the demonstration that God does not exist. As long as senseless suffering and dehumanization go on, there can be no talk of the triumph of good over evil. It was never true, and will never be true. The betrayal by institutional religion consists in promising suffering men that some day good will overcome. And so Bunuel demolishes the distinction between good and evil by reversing them, destroying the myth of moral certitude and replacing it with a deeply cynical moral ambiguity. This appears to be a very dark portrait of human existence, but, as we shall see, it has its meanings for those who share a faith Bunuel seems to have abandoned.

4

The Banality of Evil:
Bunuel's Cinematic Style

There is a disconcerting tendency, after viewing a Bunuel film, to discuss Bunuel rather than the film. This may be a tribute to the man's ability to put so much of himself into his works, but it is also a comment on his unique cinematic style. It is strangely difficult to analyze Bunuel's techniques because he achieves his revelations without drawing attention to his craft. Critics frequently refer to the directness and economy of his narrative, his speed in working, and his sangfroid camera work. However, few analysts relate these qualities to Bunuel's attitudes toward good and evil in the world. It is for this reason that I have devoted the following pages to reflection on the basic effect of his bland style, which is to underline the banality of evil. We can explore this idea in considering Bunuel's films in terms of their aesthetic iconoclasm, their stylistic humanism, their moral ambiguity, and their finely wrought surrealism. The result should be to balance our previous emphasis upon his thematic preoccupations with an awareness of how completely Bunuel's style reflects his conceptions.

Bunuel has said, "I put into my films what I want to put in them." This remark must be believed. However, it is not so much a reference to content as it is a comment on style. Most of his films, after all, have been adapted

178

from the works of others, including such classics as
Wuthering Heights and *The Adventures of Robinson Crusoe*. What makes these adaptations uniquely his own is
Bunuel's ability to film them within his own moral and
aesthetic universe. There is always the feeling that Bunuel
has made his point, but, as we shall see, this does not
mean he has created arguments in film. Rather, he has
fashioned environments clearly reflecting his vision of
man, society, and reality.

There is a sense in which Bunuel has not changed his
style from 1928 to the present, except to become more
terse, swift, and accurate in his communications. Although scenes from *L'Age d'Or, Los Olvidados, Viridiana*
and *Belle de Jour* are frequently beautiful in their mood,
lighting, and composition, these films reveal no attempt
to create lyrical beauty as such. The overt aesthetic
iconoclasm of *Un Chien Andalou* set the tone, with its
abandonment of plot, characterization, or any of the
purely narrative unities. But gradually Bunuel turned to
an episodic narrative style, as in the picaresque structure
of *Milky Way* or *Nazarin*. His films do tell a "story," but
the point of his artistic rebellion is that the "story" is not
what these films are about. In this respect, Bunuel has
maintained an enviable independence. When television
generated a taste for closeups, Bunuel still favored medium shots. When Welles and later Fellini, Bergman, and
others turned to deep-focus photography and rich shad-
ows, Bunuel stuck to somewhat flat lighting and ordinary
lenses. His one concession to modernity was to use color
in *Belle de Jour* and subsequent films, but like other
aspects of his craft, he seems to have mastered color on
his first try. The shiny palette of *Belle*, for example,
perfectly suits her child's world of fantasy, just as the
muted tones of Toledo's back streets suit the somber
motives of *Tristana*. Similarly, the gospel sequences of
The Milky Way are immediately recognizable by their
nineteenth-century religious painting style and coloring.
But Bunuel was able to accomplish the same recognition

in his black and white representation of Jesus in the blasphemous Chateau de Selligny episode of *L'Age d'Or*, a perfect replica of inferior religious movies. The point is that gratuitous aesthetics repel Bunuel, and he often goes out of his way to associate them with Fascism or decadence.

Bunuel's stylistic nonconformism has an ideological basis—it is in fact an attack on the hidden presumption that some things in this world are beautiful and others are not; that one face is worth looking at, and another is not; that some human actions and situations are beautiful, while others are intrinsically ugly. In effect, Bunuel asks us to look at them all, to see them wholly, and to appreciate in them the basic humanity that is always present. It is in this sense that we shall refer to his stylistic humanism, which is totally different from other vaunted humanisms that dignify a degrading humanitarianism. Bunuel's camera is the key to his style; it is an accepting eye which drinks in the world of objects and men without blinking at deformity and without winking at a superior viewer.

The first impression one gets of a Bunuel film is of its extreme concreteness. The surfaces of his films are filled with objects: the clutter of Crusoe's caveful of salvaged civilization; the affluent appointments of the drawing room abused in *Exterminating Angel;* the treasured possessions which Don Lope sells and then regains in *Tristana.* Bunuel's early works make it clear that this "thingedness" of existence has a symbolic-psychological significance in his films. We have seen his characters dragging objects out of their psyche, or tossing them out of the chambers of their mind. In recent films he has worked metaphorically with whole locations and interiors, carefully conceiving them to externalize the world views of his characters. The decaying refinements of Don Jaime's parlor are a significant example, as is the monastic decor of Viridiana's room. And Bunuel's camera notes everything.

The viewer attuned to Bunuel's style can receive a strong set of sensory impressions for each person or locale. The object reveals the character, be it as simple as Simon's food pouch or as exotic as Viridiana's crown of thorns. Equally important, but much less commented upon, are the tactile qualities of Bunuel's costuming, locations, and actions. Hands are featured caressing, stroking, or striking. A woman rubs her leg and thighs with milk, or an egg yolk; a dove's breast is stroked across a woman's back, in a superstitious attempt at healing. The smells of man's animal nature are evoked in barns and in salons such as that of *Exterminating Angel,* where the camera or a casual word makes them overpoweringly real. Taste fascinates Bunuel in a special way, perhaps because it is so primitive a sense. Eating, for example, marks our basic humanity, especially in the strong peasant type who represents his sanity by tending to needs for food, just as the pilgrims of *Milky Way* are so often seen eating. The basic metaphor in *The Discreet Charm of the Bourgeoisie* is a meal never completed except in the fantasies of the gourmet couples. The equanimity with which they pursue this elusive dinner through innumerable obstacles is less a sign of restraint than of surfeit. Their interest in food is almost purely aesthetic . . . a refinement that might be tolerated if men were not still starving. And when they do sit at table, their eating itself becomes an absurdity, even though it is executed with impeccable manners. In the end, it is man's appetites that betray him. The ambassador's inability to resist that last cut of roast lamb leads to his arrest by the police.

Sound is also important in Bunuel's films, but its development may have been limited, through the years, by his growing deafness. *L'Age d'Or* was among the first sound films made, and yet it shows a mastery of complex sound mixing. Bunuel's films are seldom scored by a musical director, chiefly because the musical background is integral to the action. When we hear Bach or Handel in *Viridiana* it is because Don Jaime is playing the organ or the windup phonograph. Similarly, Don Jorge's radio provides the rock and roll for the closing scene of that film. Frequently, Bunuel uses classical music for its connotations of decadent aestheticism. The absurd love scene in *L'Age d'Or* is accompanied by Wagner's *Tristan and Isolde,* the surging music allowed to contrast with the frustrated grapplings. The music has a greater impact for being used sparingly, as in the sensual surrender of the rock and roll in *Viridiana* or the "Radioactive Flesh" dance in *Simon of the Desert.* The wind, a barking dog, a drumroll (at the end of *Nazarin*), or carriage bells—each signifies a moment of drama or decision. But the strongly evocative sensory impressions of Bunuel's films tend to be presented somewhat statically; Bunuel allows only a small role to kinetic impressions in his film. Rarely do we follow rapidly moving objects, and when the camera does search a scene, it does so unobtrusively, and almost invisibly.

Though all the senses mentioned are important, it is the eye that responds most to Bunuel's style. Most of his metaphors are visual, and the probing-eye camera style itself becomes a metaphor of his philosophy of man. Critics note that Bunuel admires and uses the medium shot style of the American action directors of the forties, a technique that cut down on camera setups and permitted a swift flow of narrative. Certainly it is true that he uses what has been called the "head to knees" shot, grouping his characters so that their relations to one another and to the environment become clear in a glance. Occasionally a medium shot, but almost never a closeup, appears to break the pattern which consciously distances us from his characters. The impact of this style is to make the viewer a mere observer, one who can scrutinize the actions and people from an analytical perspective. For example, Bunuel seldom singles out his primary characters by closeups, preferring instead to use careful compositions and subtle dialogue to emphasize their importance. Again, the result is a natural unfolding of relationships, but it is always achieved at the price of a conscious noninvolvement in the characters' lives.

The coldness and detachment with which Bunuel's characters are treated has often been attributed to the director's lack of concern. Yet Bunuel cares enough for his characters, after all, to show all kinds of men, and to record their desires, weaknesses, and sufferings honestly. But he does not invite you to match your experience with theirs—to identify with them. Most audiences find the lives of Bunuel characters somewhat bizarre, if not outlandish. Bunuel is desperately concerned to head off the rush of sympathy which his portraits of human misery might otherwise occasion. For him, pity is a form of patronizing gratification, a masturbatory congratulation that we are not as other men. He is more interested in rebellion than in charity or any other measure which alleviates human misery only long enough to blunt its cutting edge or to relieve the pressure of potential for revolution. He alienates his audience, but not in the Brechtian mode of direct insult and accusation, since he is not interested in establishing guilt or preaching a sermon. Nevertheless, the suffering we witness in his films must affect us, even at our stylistic distance. And when it does, it has a far greater impact because it is we ourselves who have allowed it to reach us.

These observations may jar against Bunuel's known delight in shocking his audiences. Of course, his tactics have become more subtle since the open outrages of *Un Chien Andalou* and *L'Age d'Or*. But there remain enough traumas to raise the question anew. We are shocked to see Jaibo murder Pedro in *Los Olvidados;* or to see Don Jaime actually smile as he plans to hold onto Viridiana by his suicide; or to see the cultured guests of *Exterminating Angel* so easily shed the veneer of civilization. What we must do is consider the motives for our outrage at the banality of evil so casually recorded by Bunuel's accepting camera eye. If we gasp, it may be because we unconsciously expected a moral comment on the evil, a judgment that neither Bunuel's camera nor his characters ever make. Frequently, it is our expectations that are frustrated. When the muscular oriental guest leaves Belle's room, the camera discovers Belle's fragile body lying face down on the bed, and we expect the worst. But when she lifts her head, we are shocked to see on her face only smiling satisfaction. However perverse the sexual experience may have been, it was pleasurable. Some of these paradoxes are never resolved. After Nazarin leaves the road gang, he hears the shots, smiles quizzically and moves on. We see Jaibo sleep with Pedro's mother, receiving the love she has withheld from her son—"so what?" the bland camera style asks. Bizarre reversals, horrendous perversities, and paradoxes of character are all alike portrayed with a complete, matter-of-fact objectivity that shocks many audiences.

Once again we must ask why we react with shock. Is it perhaps because evil is not punished as we expected, or perhaps not even labeled as evil? There is a trap set for us in the shock tactics of this anarchical artist. As in the case of the misshapen creatures who turn some of his films into a freak show, we have to ask if they repel us because we consider them less than human. Do we not wish they didn't exist, or at least were not so visible? Are we shaken by such perversities themselves as the old man's foot fetish, or are we disturbed rather by the fact that, like Joseph's brutal rape-murder in *Diary of a Chambermaid,* the perversities go unpunished? Bunuel's stylistic humanism, as we have chosen to call it, shocks us because it refuses to romanticize the misery of humanity. In most films, a child's death is savored for its emotional power by director and audience alike. If we expect this treatment, we are shocked to be deprived of it, but Bunuel says in effect that sympathy does not bring the child back or insure that another child will not die the same way. To prove his point, he presents the death without comment. Often we search for someone to care for or some way to indulge our pity in his films, but we cannot.

Are we closer to Don Lope (who seduces Tristana) or to Tristana (who destroys Don Lope)? During the agonies of *The Exterminating Angel* is there anyone we hope will preserve his humanity? Should we weep over Simon's rejection of his mother? Not at all, Bunuel says, because she's doing fine without him. And so he continues to affirm, paradoxically, the human, emphasizing what is not acknowledged as human by us: the perverse, the deformed, the amoral, the dehumanized, the unjudged, the ugly, and the unlovable. There is no nostalgia, no sentimentality, no romanticism. It is the process of life that he is feverishly exploring, and Bunuel does not dwell on any single aspect long enough to make a comment, be it moral or artistic.

The moral ambiguity that results from this style makes Bunuel's films a thorn in the side of many critics and viewers. One reason we tend to analyze Bunuel rather than the film is that we want to know how he feels about what he shows. We want him to make a comment, a judgment with his camera and script, but he does not. Our expectations are created by our education, and by a culture that favors films that never leave any doubt as to their attitudes. But Bunuel takes another tack. He says much by what he shows us, and by the way in which he reveals it, but he will not comment upon what he shows. His "no comment" is doubly paradoxical for one who is so patently a moralist, but it separates Bunuel from those moralizing directors who feel compelled to categorize every emotion and action for their audiences. Don Jaime's attempt to ravish Viridiana in her drugged state is one of the most emotionally explosive scenes in the cinema. And yet, neither in this scene nor in the earlier pathetic transvestite episode do we despise the uncle as a moral monster. We are denied outrage, laughter, superiority of any kind, and if we indulge in pity, we become part of the perversity.

Instead of moral judgment, Bunuel substitutes an ironic visual comment or a grotesque dramatic flourish.

When Beatriz is being taken off by her violent lover, they pass Nazarin without even seeing him; when Pedro's friends are carrying his body to the refuse heap, his mother passes without knowing how close she is to her son. We might seethe more over Joseph's escape from a murder charge if it were not that Celestine, shortly after she fails to expose him, marries without love the old soldier next door. And it is only upon reflection that we notice how Jorge saves Viridiana from rape only by encouraging one of the beggars to murder the other. At the time, we were probably thirsty for the rapist's blood ourselves. Not many audiences can live in this climate of moral ambiguity, and so they take revenge by accusing the director of immorality. But it is one thing to attack moral values, and another to unsettle our moral convictions by grinding away at their hidden presuppositions. It seems clear that Bunuel takes the latter path.

One of the presuppositions most challenged by Bunuel is the unspoken assumption that the world is an orderly place, man a rational creature, society a meaningful human structure, and life an ennobling experience. This "logic" of existence is for Bunuel a kind of ontological innocence, and like all innocence highly destructive of men. Bunuel is most opposed to the common views of man's rationality, and so is eager to shatter these deceptive appearances by unleashing in his films the contents of the unconscious. In his early films, the denial of logic was direct, traumatic, a frontal assault; in his later works another "logic" is substituted, resembling free association. Like the psychoanalyst who permits his client to express the most horrifying desires and emotions without guilt, Bunuel allows his camera to discover these nightmare images without comment. This tolerance is very much a part of the continuity of his films, and it is largely created by his skillful editing. A direct cut from Viridiana's ascetical practices to a cow being milked creates a shock association which is then fulfilled by her acute discomfort at having to touch anything so fleshly (obscene? phallic?) as a cow's udder. This example may be obvious, but the relational unity of a Bunuel film escapes easy analysis, building one association on another, an outrageous elliptical cut here and a treacherous dissolve there, creating relationships which we are not always willing to notice or acknowledge.

In this regard, even Bunuel's most naive, rhetorical cutaways have their function. In *Viridiana,* the cat pounces on a mouse as Jorge seduces the infatuated servant, Ramona—more a visual joke than a symbol. The boar that routs a rabbit during the rape-murder in *Diary of a Chambermaid* comments on man's animal nature. In this respect, the cutaways do not render judgment but, as it were, absolve the human beings involved. The recurring insect motif generates weird parallels with man's life, and the very pervasiveness of insect life refutes man's conviction that the earth is his or that life on the rational level rules all other. Occasionally a character will "rescue" an insect—a bee floating in a water barrel—but like the dog purchased by Jorge, one imperiled life will follow another. All is the same, Bunuel seems to say, and man's life is no different.

We have spoken of the aesthetic nonconformism, the stylistic humanism, and the moral ambiguity of Bunuel's films. All of these are part of the guiding principle and structural context of Bunuel's work, his lifelong commitment to surrealism:

> It was surrealism which showed me that life has a moral direction which man cannot but follow. For the first time I understood that man was not free. I already believed in the total liberty of man, but in Surrealism I found a discipline to follow. It was a great lesson in my life. It was also a great step forward into the marvelous and the poetic.

The Surrealist movement originated in a revolt against representational art. This disenchantment was due only partially to the invention of photography, with the dominance it gave to representational visual experience. More basically, the Surrealist revolt attacked the fallacy that truth lay in recognizability, or that "realism" required perspective and other optical techniques for its rendition. To counteract the tyranny of the actual, Surrealists (under the guidance of a misunderstood Freud) unleashed the archfoe of reason, the irrational contents of the psyche. This reversal of the rational was like the playback of events that finally released the trapped aristocrats in *Exterminating Angel*, an incantation which had the power to remove the incubus of repressive sexuality.

Some of the catchwords of the movement come as no surprise: "freedom," "total liberty," and the phrase used by Bunuel above, "a great step forward into the marvelous and the poetic." But we are not prepared to associate with Surrealism the concepts of "moral direction" and "discipline," and their centrality should be emphasized. For Bunuel the revelation of a super-real under the surface of the real was a formal structure that gave value to his creative life. It was a force that shaped his endless resources of outrage and gave them artistic expression. What might have become grubby, realistic documentaries and rhetorical filmic harangues became instead wonderful fantasies and waking nightmares, filled with imaginative devices. Even the shock tactics which marked Surrealism's attempt to shake the artistic establishment mellowed, as we have suggested, into a bland acceptance of the extraordinary. The major shock to the viewer is to realize that for Bunuel nothing is shocking. The truly surreal aspect of his art is his acceptance of all that is traditionally repellent as a casual part of existence

Surrealism is so perfectly assimilated to Bunuel's vision that it invests every scene of his films, turning them into sunny, waking nightmares. The technique was first introduced in *Las Hurdes*, where the very concreteness of his semidocumentary treatment of misery generated a hallucinatory vision of hopelessness. Ever sensitive to the secret mastery exercised by the unconscious, Bunuel seized the potential of works such as *The Exterminating*

Angel, where the paralysis of the group of nobles recalls a dream from which we achingly struggle to awaken. Occasionally a nightmare is introduced to indicate the proximity of this frightening dream world. In *Los Olvidados,* slow motion and low-key lighting turn Pedro's dream longings into a hideous caricature of motherly concern. Bunuel's characters seem to walk in the dream which is their own unreal world, like the indefatigable dinnergoers in *The Discreet Charm of the Bourgeoisie.* Viridiana is a sleepwalker through most of her life. Her symbolic entry of Uncle Jaime's room to scatter his bed with ashes is conjured up, as it were, by his nightly ritual of wearing his dead bride's wedding garments. In the rape attempt, Don Jaime and Viridiana are both drugged, he by the lifelong fantasy of his frustrated love. Simon of the Desert torments his body by fasts until he cannot separate fantasy and reality, and so he lives on the borderline, just as his pillar perch stands between heaven and earth, belonging to neither realm. And so the surreal vision goes, up to Tristana, whose nightmare visions of Uncle Lope's decapitated head serving as a church-bell clapper become the prelude to her active role in his destruction.

Dream is always becoming reality, and reality is forever yielding up its dream content. The recurring nightmare of the six friends in *The Discreet Charm of the Bourgeoisie* is to be machine-gunned to death by rebels while at dinner—a scene very nearly re-created in the police raid that ends the film. Finally, the delicate line between the two, the tender membrane between dream and reality, is ruptured, and they become one. Traditionalists may say this means insanity, but for Bunuel's surrealism it means liberation, freedom from the necessity of forever separating the real into inner dream and outer reality. Bunuel's virtuoso performance in this lifetime ambition of a surreal ideal is *Belle de Jour.* The very name conjures up images of a waking dream, a lived fairytale in which the imagined, clandestine delights of one's alter ego become daylight realities. Bunuel fragments the narrative of the film into so many levels that the very notion of discrete meanings disappears. A minimal interpretation of the story would limit the action to an evening shared by Severine and her husband, Pierre, with everything else reduced to guilt fantasies stemming from her frigid denial of sex. The other extreme would take almost all the film's action literally, with a few excursions into the past and into fantasy for the purpose of explaining Severine's character. Bunuel does nothing to dissipate the confusion, but he has scattered a few bread crumbs, suggestions quickly gobbled up by a mind ravenous for certainties after a diet of ambiguity. The point is, however, that there is no necessity to unscramble the contrasting elements of *Belle de Jour*, since Bunuel is trying to teach us to live with the unreconciled polarities in our own existence.

On the psychological level, Belle De Jour is a victim of masochistic guilt fantasies brought on by childhood experiences in which she was molested by a workman, and also forced by guilt to reject Communion. Rendered sexually frigid by her past, Severine cannot respond to Pierre, and in her guilt over this refusal she conjures up fantasies of brutal rapes and beatings by coachmen who take his orders. Immature in sexual matters, she is fascinated by the clandestine brothel, going there so she can live out consciously the self-abusing fantasies of her daydreams. But Mme. Anais' establishment strangely resembles her childhood. The Madame imposes a schoolmarm's discipline, and the guests play absurdly perverse games with the prostitutes. Severine, as may be expected, enjoys her afternoons as Belle, but we may be surprised to learn that they actually increase her love and acceptance of Pierre. The ultimate abasement of self comes in her ties to Marcel, the criminal, since her guilt has an aggressive side which can be satisfied only by dominating a dangerous man. Marcel's possessiveness, however, threatens her marriage and leads to Pierre's paralysis and the thug's death. Once again, satisfaction takes strange forms, and

Belle seems delighted to serve a husband who is almost a vegetable, but who will no longer make sexual demands on her.

All of this psychological analysis is plausible enough and would be adequate to justify a balance between fantasy and reality were it not for the alternate endings of *Belle de Jour.* These options shake our conviction about what was real and unreal in the early parts of the film. When Pierre learns from Husson that Severine has been unfaithful, he either (1) dies, after shedding a solitary tear, or (2) is cured of paralysis and restored to his wife and to a stable, healthy relationship. But the jingle of carriage bells, which introduced other excursions into dream, come to remind us that fantasy is never far away, even if the coach this time passes by unoccupied.

In *Belle de Jour* the moral ambiguity of Bunuel's ideology merges with the ontological ambiguity of surrealism. The film is the fulfillment of the ideals of Andre Breton, theorist of the Surrealist movement:

> Everything leads us to believe that there exists a certain point of the spirit at which life and death, the real and the imaginary, the past and the future . . . cease to be perceived as opposites. It is vain to see in the Surrealists' activity any motive other than the location of that point.[1]

Bunuel seems to have reached that elusive point, and this realization helps us to understand not only works like *Belle* and *Tristana,* but all his films. They are all alike surreal: from the concrete social situations of *Los Olvidados* to the abstract episodes of *The Milky Way;* from the semi-allegory of *The Exterminating Angel* to the reverse romanticism of *Tristana.* The strange poetry of Bunuel's images derives from this intentional confusion that destroys artificial distinctions. At once we can see the reconciliation of the paradoxes in his work. He can be a stylistic humanist because he is determined to reveal

1. Quoted without reference by Durgnat, *Luis Bunuel,* p. 140.

the basic humanity below what is apparently subhuman. He can communicate moral outrage without rhetorical harangue because the change for which he longs goes beyond conversion—it aims for nothing short of an annihilating insight. And he can break or ignore artistic convention because his own formal credo is calculated to destroy any convention that obscures clear vision. The cool yet fanatical zeal with which Bunuel has pursued this meta-surrealism has given his films an ironically "religious" fervor. If we need any argumentation on that score, we need only quote the words of the master surrealist himself:

> If only the white eyelid of the screen reflected its proper light, the Universe would go up in flames, but for the time being, we can sleep in peace . . . the light of the cinema is conveniently ossified and shackled.

Although Bunuel's images and actions have grown more calm and dignified, this manifesto has lost none of its bitterness over the years. Bunuel is still a crusader for a private cause that has in a sense already been won. The banality of evil is demonstrated stylistically in Bunuel's films, in terms that help us recognize its multiple interventions in our own history. The filmmaker, unlike the ineffectual preacher, has demonstrated to the perceptive viewer that viewer's own complicity in dehumanizing processes, but without resorting to moral abstractions, motivations of guilt, or simplistic personifications of our impulses and desires. This process of cleansing enlightenment we recognize today as a remarkable work of demythologizing. Bunuel has anticipated and has provided the artistic counterpart of the theological movement culminating in the Death of God.

5

The Gospel According to Bunuel

In *The Milky Way,* the pilgrims en route to Santiago de Compostella argue over faith. Hoping to convert the believer, the atheist steps out into a thunderstorm and challenges God to strike him dead with lightning. Nothing happens. But as he returns jubilant to the shelter, a lightning bolt strikes a hundred yards away. God is late, and he has a bad aim.

This is the Gospel according to Bunuel, a tract concerned less with proving the nonexistence than the nonnecessity of God. In other words, by attacking the myths about God and man patiently, systematically, thoroughly, Bunuel is among the first of our contemporaries to announce the Death of God. The precision and insight with which the director forwards this project force us to reject other, superficial labels for his work. Instead of a reckless anarchist, a dirty old man, or a chronic malcontent anticlerical, Bunuel is a skilled demythologizer, announcing the passing of the deity in ways that closely parallel the recent work of a generation of theologians.

Some of the earliest images in Bunuel's films reveal his function as demythologizer (then considered as iconoclast), and these scenes become a metaphor for his life work. The razor in *Un Chien Andalou* is like a scalpel wielded by a skilled surgeon, determined to open our eyes to the harsh realities we have encrusted with debili-

tating myths. The instrument is precise in excising patho-
logical tissue, and its efficacy in Bunuel's hands may be
therapeutic as in medicine. Like the deadly sting of the
scorpion in *L'Age d'Or*, Bunuel's cinematic images can
kill within us a god who is more the product of our own
idolatry than the supreme personal source of freedom
and love. And it is true, as in *Las Hurdes*, that the remedy
we sometimes apply to the sting of Bunuel's criticism is
more toxic than the bite. Stinging critic and skilled surgeon, Bunuel's camera moves through the maze of culturally conditioned belief like a fanatic prophet announcing not the imminence of God's judgment, but the threat
of human freedom. The tools of Bunuel's craft as demythologizer are taken from his education and culture,
religious rituals and images which he is compelled to use
even as he destroys them. However, under the lens of his
pervasive surrealism, in the furnace of his perduring
rage, these sexual and religious images are forged into
profound analogies, into striking visual metaphors of the
human condition in our day.

"I intend to show, with a cold, white eye, what they
have done here on earth in the name of God," Bunuel has
said. Luis Bunuel's cold, white eye is directed like a laser
beam at the actions of believers whose deeds belie their
faith and prove that God does *not* exist. This function
places Bunuel in the company of theologians who, with
equal improbability, have turned to the work of stripping
away the myths from our notions of God. Although
many names are associated with this movement in theology, its origins can be traced to the writings of Paul
Tillich, Karl Barth, and Dietrich Bonhoeffer, while its
controversial formulations are to be found in the works
of Thomas Altizer, Paul Van Buren, and William Hamilton. While many theologians have commented upon the
debate, Harvey Cox has given a systematic overview of
the field well suited to our purposes. I hope to use his
synthesis as proof that Luis Bunuel is the cinematic

predecessor of the Death of God theology which domi-
nated the scene a few years ago.[1]

Tracing the controversy back to Paul Tillich's mistrust
of the term "is" when applied to God, Harvey Cox
couples this reservation with Karl Barth's doctrines on
christology to establish the two as predecessors of the
Death of God movement. If we were to add to this
Dietrich Bonhoeffer's "coming of age," the realization
that we must do without God, then the background for
the movement is more or less complete. Out of this
matrix arose the Death of God, a concept which, as Cox
points out, has at least three meanings, each of them
associated with a key theologian. Briefly, the phrase
"Death of God" can mean that it is futile to say anything
about "God," or that our culturally conditioned ways of
experiencing God have deteriorated, or that communications (religious language and symbol) have made the word
"God" ambiguous. As we shall see, Bunuel proves to be a
skilled demythologizer in each of the three categories.

Positivism provides a methodology for Paul Van
Buren's claim that the word "God" has no visible empirical referent, and that "Christianity is about man and not
about God." Thomas Altizer is equally nontheistic, but
his reliance upon Buddhist and Hegelian ideas moves him
to propose another claim, that the real, transcendent
God, who became immanent in Jesus, actually died in the
crucifixion. To realize this, he says, is to have an insight
resembling religious conversion, and it provides a motive
for proclamation. Cultural analysis, on the other hand,
follows Tillich in noting that technological change and
urbanization have punctured the cultural "envelope" in
which we have hitherto experienced God. If the reality of
God is identical with the experience of God, then wher-

1. Harvey Cox, "The Death of God and the Future of Theology," in
New Theology, No. 4, ed. Martin Marty & Dean G. Peerman (New York:
Macmillan, 1967), pp. 243-253, is the source for portions of the following
theological survey.

ever he is no longer experienced he may be considered literally dead. Cox himself, however, posits a crisis in communications, in which the term "God" is given so many meanings that God might as well be dead for all that our invocation of his name can do.

Bunuel has approached his task of demythologizing a post-Christian culture from each of these directions, at times generating a kind of mystical atheism, at other times proposing empirical refutations of faith, and at still other times analyzing the cultural ramifications of God's existence to find it a destructive, dehumanizing force. I hope to show that in each of these three directions the director retains the surgeon's touch, and the scorpion's sting.

Luis Bunuel has often been accused of atheistic humanism. The fact that the charge is either unjustified or strongly in need of qualification does not alter the fact that it is made frequently. Therefore, it must be faced as the first level of his lifetime project of demythologization. If Paul Van Buren can declare impatiently that "Christianity is about man and not God," then Bunuel can provide images and actions which reveal the injustice of talking about God when men suffer. Even where Bunuel seems to take real concern for man as a criterion of religious zeal, there is little doubt as to the direction (God or man) that he favors. The paradox, however, is that he tends to attack the question on religious grounds, that is, in terms of traditional religious questions, of believers, church structures, and theological problems, even in terms of religious symbolism—all of which he manages to turn on its head to make his point. Bunuel's "atheistic humanism," therefore, is a unique and "unorthodox" form of that persuasion, a fact that is most evident in Bunuel's images of God and Christ and in his disillusionment with Christianity.

The essence of Bunuel's eccentric atheism is summed up in the opening scene of *The Milky Way*. The two vagabond pilgrims meet a stranger who refuses alms to

the penniless one, but gives to the other, who already has
something (a direct reference to the Gospel). Then, de-
livering a harsh prophecy, the man walks off with a dwarf
who releases a white dove—Bunuel's own bizarre and
blasphemous Trinity. However, Bunuel has filmed other
images of God, and especially of Christ, beginning with
Jesus portrayed as the Count de Blangis in the *Hundred
Days of Sodom* episode at the end of *L'Age d'Or*. The
shock value of this image proved to be limited, and so
Bunuel's next reference was more veiled: in the "Last
Supper" orgy of *Viridiana*, the place of Christ is taken by
Don Amalio, the most violent and vicious of the lot. In
another approach, the host, Nobile, in *Exterminating
Angel*, is a Christ-figure so patronizing and ineffectual
that he removes his jacket so the boorishness of the other
guests won't be so apparent. And when Sylvia Pinal
appears as a marcelled "Lamb of God" in *Simon of the
Desert*, we recognize the derisive thrust of the image.

Critics and analysts seldom reflect on the form of these
"revelations," which almost always find a base for their
representations of God and Christ in religious paintings,
that is, our own images of the deity. The "Jesus" of
L'Age d'Or is immediately recognized by his appearance
and by the eyes rolled up to heaven—all of which is the
heritage of the dreadful biblical films of the time. The
double-edged menace of this black humor is apparent: if
we react in shock to the portrait, Bunuel could rightly
ask if we assume our recognition of the Savior from the
compromised portrait he has chosen. Similarly, the Gospel episodes of *The Milky Way* are meticulously done in
the palette of Hoffman and other nineteenth-century
"religious" painters. Most notorious of all, the *Last Supper* of Leonardo da Vinci provides the inspiration for the
traumatic recognition towards the end of *Viridiana*. However, recalling that this is a surgeon and not a cartoonist
operating, we should probe beneath the surface of these
images. Why did Bunuel choose this "Last Supper"?
Perhaps because it is in direct opposition to the event,

focusing as it does upon the moment of betrayal summarized in the words, "Is it I, Lord?" A fact that believers may miss does not escape Bunuel's attention. His scene is a moment of betrayal, and the complex interrelations of the crude band of intruders reveal that the essential ingredient of the Gospel event—the prodigal pouring out of God's love for man in Christ—is missing. Similarly, we should be reluctant to claim the Jesus of *L'Age d'Or* as our own, especially since the "sting" of this scene bears upon the repressive use of religion to create the bizarre parodies of love that are the subject of the Marquis de Sade's writings. Even the callow camaraderie of the "hippy" Christ of *Milky Way* finds its target—the Jesus Revolution, which for some consists in making Jesus a street radical, a cultural rebel, a typical counter-culture hero fascinated with his own rhetoric.

Direct or indirect, serious or burlesque, these representations of God and Christ are our own idealized distortions of reality, visual myths with which we surround the Deity. And Bunuel incisively reveals the human accretions on reality by attacking them with his unique venom. But in each attack, there is a valuable insight. How deeply one must understand St. John's Gospel in order to stage an orgy like that of *Viridiana!* Even where the subject matter is not directly religious, we can see the jugular thrust. Is it not possible, for example, that in *Belle de Jour* Severine (the very name is a sentence!) represents the Church's distorted love of Christ, a sado-masochistic charade which willingly accepts him as a paralyzed cripple?

Behind the scalpel strokes and the scorpion's sting, there is a frustrated expectation. God, after all, is always on *their* side, on the side of the exploiters who dehumanize and kill. Hard work and honesty are not rewarded in *Los Olvidados*, they are destroyed without retaliation— God does not intervene. And in *Diary of a Chambermaid*, a crucifix hangs on the wall of the rapist-murderer, as it will in the political headquarters of his fascist party. Is it not true, furthermore, that the Eucharist has become for some the moral litmus-paper test of serious sin, as it is in *Belle*'s flashback to childhood guilt? Bunuel seems to be crying in exasperation, "When will God be on the side of man?" From this implicit question, it is easy to deduce his own humanism, the plea so evident in *The Milky Way*—stop questioning and discoursing on God and begin attending to basic human needs! Bunuel, in his own words, has been showing us what men have done here on earth "in the name of God," and his solution is to stop invoking God's name. It is the same proposal made by several of the Death of God theologians. Christ has become a charm, our fetish, bolted to the dashboard of our cars, nailed to our walls, tied on a golden chain about our necks—his name mouthed by politicians who give their approval to massacres. If he *is* God, then his death will not be mourned by the likes of Luis Bunuel.

After each thrust at God, Bunuel turns to human needs. In this, he seems to parallel the cultural analysis of theologians such as Gabriel Vahanian. If the images of Christ drawn by Bunuel demolish a domesticated myth, then his character portraits of the Imitators of Christ attack the supposed humanist benefits of the Christian life. It is interesting that they do so from the sad perspective of the frustrated ideal. In the words of Bunuel, "One can be *relatively* Christian, but the absolute pure being, the innocent, is condemned to defeat. He is beaten in advance." This remark, made in justification of Nazarin, applies to Bunuel's portraits of other exemplary Christians. Simon of the Desert is not treated harshly, but he is easiest to dismiss. The monk reminds him that his life is of little value to man—Bunuel's ultimate criterion. Viridiana apparently does not want a life of service, but a "community" of which she can be Mother Superior, the absolute power. And even if this is reflex Christianity—religious impulse flowing into rigid, institutional channels that make every mission impersonal—the realization does not help the beggars. Nazarin is perhaps the most complex

of all, favored as he is by Bunuel as a man in his "moral
line." But in spite of his efforts, Nazarin fails, his innocence
a destructive force that leaves things worse than he
found them. The paradox of Nazarin is that he appears to
have chosen the humanist approach to the Christian mission. But the choice is only apparent. Like Viridiana, he
is not completely human. He is as cold as the snail which
rests in his hand as he lectures Andara and Beatriz (who
love him humanly) on the superiority of "universal love."
The popular sarcasm, "I must love all men, because I
don't love anyone in particular," applies tragically to
Nazarin. Any human love, Bunuel seems to say, is superior to this abstraction, this universal love that is love
stripped of all its human features. Even Pinto's fierce,
exploitative possession of Beatriz outweighs Nazarin's
detached concern. The same is true of Nazarin's attempt
to compete with the physical comfort of the plague
victim's lover. Most sublime of all is the love of Ujo, the
dwarf, for Andara—a grotesque, hopeless, but unforgettable passion.

Bunuel takes special care to destroy this myth of a
"spiritual" universal love superior to the human. He does
so by showing the deficient humanity of the imitators of
Christ, of people such as Simon, Viridiana, and Nazarin.
To the extent that they deny their humanity, they give
less than human comfort to those they serve. The dead
weight of the clerics dragged along in *Un Chien Andalou*
measures their contribution to sexual repression and perversion. The Carmelite monastery abandoned in *Las
Hurdes* has been repossessed by the scorpions. In *Subida
al Cielo* it is the village without a priest that thrives; the
one served by a cleric is in trouble. The worker-bishop
makes no impact on the lives of the bourgeoisie—like
them, he exists and survives on his "discreet charm."
There was a time when these Christians would have been
respected, when their lives might even be effective, but
that time is past. The cultural soil in which they grew is
badly eroded, residual Christendom is imperiled, and the

experience of God is becoming a faded memory. For Bunuel, the God that once provided, nay, constituted, this experience, is dead.

The defeat of the crucifixion was for Bunuel, as for certain theologians today, definitive: "Christ was crucified after being condemned. Don't you think that was a defeat? . . . I'm sure that if Christ returned, the preachers, the Church, would condemn him." And yet there is always the question behind Bunuel's remarks, the reservation behind his images. Christianity is there, an impossible ideal rendered ineffectual, but *there*. The reason why it fails, apparently, is its betrayal of its own promise toward the human, a betrayal for which Bunuel cannot summon any adequate forgiveness: "I look with affection on everyone. One is good, not very good, good mixed with bad. . . . I love them all. I love people, and show them as they are because I love them."

Those shocked by the procession of vicious, diseased, perverted, deformed humanity that courses through Bunuel's films will react with outrage to the director's protestation of love for all men. But perhaps the key to Bunuel's love is his willingness to "show them as they are," that is, to refuse to participate in any myth of physical beauty or original innocence that can blind us to man's failings. He has seen the outcome of this myth based on religious grounds—it is to love only those who are "good" and to leave others outside the circle of human concern. Prisoners, foreigners, the ugly, diseased or deformed, the poor, can easily become the victims of moral judgments concerning their responsibility for their predicament. Bunuel has seen this selective Christianity in action, and he finds in it an implicit rejection of the human that challenges the impact of the Incarnation.

If Christianity is an impossible ideal, it is perhaps because the Incarnation has never been understood or accepted in its full implications. Bunuel's willingness to accept all humanity, the camera that does not blink, wince, or turn aside at any image or action, indicates a

strong but unusual love for man—a unique, personal humanism. The Incarnation has been conceptualized into a
Manichean Dualism, an open hostility or at least an
uneasy truce between the human and the divine, pitting
the flesh and the spirit against each other as evil against
good. Simon of the Desert, perched between heaven and
earth, not really a part of either, hardly communicating
with them, is a prototype of this harmful dichotomy.
Viridiana speaks of continuing her vocation "in the
world," but she succeeds only in converting the world
into the convent. Nazarin abandons his cassock and goes
"on the road," but he carries with him the burden of a
human denial so strong that the offer of a piece of fruit
almost destroys him.

The only hope Bunuel offers these Christians is the
rediscovery of their humanity. Viridiana will play cards
with Jorge and Ramona. They are not paragons of virtue,
but they are human, more comfortable with their humanity than she is. And, by making no judgment on his
characters, Bunuel performs a silent absolution, forgiving
them for their humanity. One is reminded of Leonard
Cohen's poem *The Sisters of Mercy*, in which men lie
down beside prostitutes to make their confession to
them. The sin of which we are all guilty, Bunuel seems to
say, is our humanity, and in order to allay the guilt, he
shows us the mixture of good and evil that is the human
condition. Those who fare best are the simple, the peasants described above, who accept their instincts and follow their natures. Is there, in this scheme, a danger of
reducing Christ to a "mere human" (a phrase that Bunuel
would find amusing)? Of course there is. Just as certain
acceptations of the human covertly limit man's potential,
some images of Christ leave no room for transcendence.
But the problem is not Bunuel's, since he is convinced
that the denial of the human is what has made Christianity an impossible ideal. The Incarnation that was to build
a bridge between God and man, between man and his

nature, has instead been turned into an unbridgeable gap separating humanity into unassimilable fragments.

The third level on which Luis Bunuel anticipates and parallels the Death of God theologians is the work of demythologizing the "religious language and symbol structure" referred to by Harvey Cox. Bunuel gives the impression of a man obsessed by religion largely because he uses the symbol structure of Christianity, almost intact, to destroy the myths encased by this structure. He is noted for his "sacred iconoclasm," but it is seldom realized that he shatters the idols with religious images and a ritualistic style. Once more we are caught in a paradox of his temperament, because a basic understanding of this symbol structure is requisite even to recognize its destruction. Bunuel's films are, on the level of form, image, visual metaphor, and ritual action, the visual gnosticism of an agnostic. We can illustrate this paradox by citing his constant return to sacred objects and to the central metaphor of the Church.

Wherever churches appear in Bunuel's films, they accompany actions or attitudes that belie their purpose. El Bruto conceives his insane passion at a Holy Thursday foot-washing ceremony in church, as if the tactile reminder of his humanity broke down the taboos of the sacred place, releasing repressed passions. Later, he almost murders another priest in a church. The Church hierarchy appears in *L'Age d'Or* as a shipwreck, the dead bishops having foundered on the rock of human needs and desires that interrupt the founding ceremony. The church in *Tristana* is the place where official witnesses confirm a marriage of vengeance between the crippled girl and her intended victim. Ultimately, all believers are trapped in their church like the cultured nobles of *Exterminating Angel*, unable to leave the web of traditions, of paralyzing rituals. Even the character of Viridiana, insofar as she symbolizes the Church, bespeaks the abuse (rape) of a sacred cultural tradition. The Bride of Christ is an effective, earthy appellation for the Church in Catholicism. When Viridiana is dressed in the wedding gown of Don Jaime's dead bride, she becomes not merely the object of his frustrated desires, but the metaphor of the Church in its relations to the state. Don Jaime, the Old Spain, has grown accustomed to using the Church to prop up its hegemony; the bastard son Jorge, the New Spain, is just as willing to exploit the Church, albeit in a more contemporary vein. In either case, the attempted rape of Viridiana is simply the age-old use of the Church to further human ambitions, an abuse which began, some would say, with Constantine's elevation of Christianity to the status of the official religion. It is not by accident that Bunuel has the "Hallelujah Chorus," from Handel's *Messiah*, playing during the orgy in *Viridiana*. Bunuel has selected a piece of triumphalist music to supply the last irony for the exploitative condition of the revelers. The white-bearded Don Zequiel, who represents St. Peter, pronounces the absolution: "Let them sin, so that their repentance is greater! Besides, it's good for the soul!"

Bunuel recounts that, as students in a religious school, he and his fellow pupils used to masturbate before a statue of the Virgin. The borderline between exploratory eroticism and emotional piety was apparently not yet clear. And yet Bunuel's films are replete with the abuse of sacred objects, a ritualistic recurrence that is almost obsessive. His sacred iconoclasm is very skillful, however, and shows remarkable insight into the objects and their functions. In *Viridiana*, the bastard son Jorge is fascinated with a crucifix that opens into a pocket knife—his father's legacy of destructive religiosity. Viridiana's own fetishes—the instruments of the Passion—are burned by the child Rita after she pricks her hand. When the monk carrying the Eucharist to Simon slips on the ladder, he drops the sacred Host and hangs on for dear life. Throughout Bunuel's films, the vicious and perverted surround themselves with religious fetishes: the religious paintings in Joseph's room, in *Diary of a Chambermaid;*

the Dali crucifixion in the Claudel-reading police chief's office, in *Cela s'Appelle l'Aurore.* Sacred vessels are turned to profane use. Fr. Lizzardi's breviary pages help light a fire in *La Mort en ce Jardin,* and his chalice becomes a drinking cup when the struggle for survival becomes more grim. The process we have noted clearly becomes an iconoclasm of the sacred, in which the holy is used to shatter the holy. Bunuel seems bent on sacralizing the "profane," even if it means abusing the sacred.

These recurring sacred images appear in patterns that take on the nature of ritual, as if Bunuel were constructing his own perverse liturgies. The rhythmic rites are evident in the barn scene of *Viridiana,* where the perversely precocious Rita pours milk on a calf's head, a reference to the magic ritual whose proscription gave rise to the Hebrew kosher laws. In *Los Olvidados,* the blind quack "cures" a woman by rubbing her back with a dove's breast; another dove is caught and its feathers scattered during the orgy in *Viridiana.* The elaborate foot fetishes in *Diary of a Chambermaid* take place with as much attention to rubrical niceties as the self-abasing sexual charades of the pathetic visitors to Mme. Anais' bordello in *Belle de Jour.* Again, the mock funeral to which the Duke invites Belle is a religious ceremony turned inside out. As always, the borderline between ritual and magic is blurred purposely by Bunuel. The trapped elite in *Exterminating Angel* must retrace their words and actions, like a prayer said backwards, before they can free themselves. Those later trapped in the church have just completed a religious ceremony which they may have to reverse in order to escape.

In reality, it is Bunuel constructing his own evil iconography for the ritual exorcism of objects and actions that obsess him. When Crusoe receives no answer to the shouted verses of the Psalm, he runs to the sea and extinguishes his flaming torch in the waves, a gesture of exorcism that may symbolize the quenching of his faith . . . or of Bunuel's. This filmic process of exorcism gathers candles, statues, and incense for the cinematic ceremony which, in seeming to celebrate evil, attempts to restore life through ritual.

The myths of religious ceremony are the major target of Bunuel's imagery. Many of them have become meaningless repetitions, superstitious fetishes which bind people, as the Hurdanos, in ignorance and in poverty. But the manner in which Bunuel excises these objects and actions elevates them to a metaphorical level. The director, as we noted, is diligent in eradicating good/evil dichotomies, destroying moralistic judgments on human weakness. In the same way, he is interested in breaking down the artificial distinctions between the sacred and the profane. His abuse of sacred objects does not simply destroy them, but reduces them to their primary (human) use. Implicit in both concept and style is the conviction that nothing is profane, a conviction that a believer's perception would expand if he recognized that the profane is what *we* separate from the sacred source, namely God. But the way Bunuel expresses this conviction befits the iconoclast. He demonstrates that everything is holy by showing that, for him, nothing is sacred. If we, in turn, gasp at his iconoclasm, it may be that we have been caught in the compromising distinction between the sacred and the profane.

The visual symbolism of Bunuel's films, which we have characterized as a "gnosticism," gives a strange, analogical depth to the films. The objects and actions which he attacks are "sacramental" in the deeper sense of the word; not that they are blessed in a ceremony, but that they signify other levels of reality through their own concrete existence. Bunuel's camera pays ritual attention to these objects as it incorporates them into his private exorcisms, the mixture of eroticism and religion that haunts his films like the smell of incense in an empty church. They are part of his surreal imagination, and the climate of free association which communicates the interrelation of all things does not leave out these consecrated objects. The notion of a more intense reality at the base of the everyday appearances is fundamentally a religious concept, and when Bunuel constructs his puzzling rituals around symbolic objects, he is fulfilling his mission of opening our eyes to levels of reality otherwise inaccessible.

In *Simon of the Desert* the devil possesses one of the monks who serve Simon, and he plants rich foods in the anchorite's pouch as evidence of his hypocrisy. When this duplicity is discovered, the other monks briskly set about exorcising the devil from their fellow, replying to his blasphemies with their own convictions until the devil utters something which they know not whether to support or reject. In confusion, one monk says, "This devil knows more theology than we do!" The devil referred to is obviously Luis Bunuel, and he proves his theological expertise in *The Milky Way,* where he sets out to eradicate theology. The process of demythologizing would not be complete without this extension to theology, and in fact *The Milky Way* attacks rational Christianity in a manner close to the more pietistic of the Death of God theologians. Many have commented upon the fact that these theologians stood in danger of putting themselves out of a job by pronouncing him dead. Bunuel creates the same effect by saturating us in theology, flooding every scene with historical and contemporary theological debate until we find so total a preoccupation with the divine absurd. His point is that theology not only has contributed to myth, but has itself become part of the myth, so that it must be checked before Christianity can reappear from under the tomes of theological debate that have stifled it for centuries. When it does reappear, Bunuel seems to promise, it may manifest a more human visage than that we now associate with it.

Since we have associated Bunuel with the work of theologians, it may be helpful to compare his work with Dietrich Bonhoeffer's interpretation of the Death of God:

So our coming of age forces us to a true recognition of our situation *vis à vis* God. God is teaching us that we must live as men who can get along very well without him. The God who is with us is the God who forsakes us (Mark 15:34). The God who makes us live in this world without using him as a working hypothesis is the God before whom we are ever standing. Before God and with him we live without God. God allows himself to be edged out of the world and on to the cross. . . .

Man's religiosity makes him look in his distress to the power of God in the world; he uses God as a *Deus ex machina.* [2]

Leaving aside the context of Bonhoeffer's faith, this statement not only could have been made by Bunuel—it *has* been made over and over again in each of his films. His characters can get along very well without God. Many of them have used God to justify their own vices and ambitions, making of him, as Bonhoeffer suggests, an escape hatch, a *Deus ex machina.* For this reason, Bunuel has announced his gospel, proclaimed the word that God is dead. We live in a post-Christian culture still obsessed by mythical remnants, vestiges of the past which carry in their tangle of legends what we once called God. Bunuel sees these myths repressing human development, and so he sets out to eradicate them. As the traditional symbols collapse, they bring down the gods with them, as is always the case in rapid social change. But it is Bunuel, the skillful surgeon, who discovers the disease. The question is, does he also uncover within his own being a living tissue of religious reality—the experience of God?

This "last of the blasphemers" demonstrates that some form of faith is necessary, even to utter a curse. His films are alive with the absence of an absolute to which by temperament he is strongly drawn. The most personal (and terrible) notice which Bunuel posts on the death of God is the news that he is no longer able to experience

2. *Letters and Papers from Prison* (New York: Macmillan, 1962), pp. 219-220.

God himself. But his search, nevertheless, very much resembles an act of blind faith. His statement on the rejection of Christ contains a strange postscript: "I'm sure that if Christ returned, the preachers, the Church, would condemn him. . . . In a world as badly made as this, the only path to take is that of rebellion." Not only does he associate the work of Christ with rebellion, but he implies that his own creative work has been an apostolate of rebellion, a protest against a world badly made. Bunuel once claimed he would have preferred to live in the Middle Ages. This is no longing for simple faith, but indicates his instinctive preference for absolutes, his nostalgia for a world which left a place for the spiritual.

God is dead, and for Bunuel that means that man is free. That is, man *can be free*. It may take a revolution to establish the freedom we radically hold, but it is there for us to seize. As Bunuel once commented on the last state of Crusoe and Friday in his *Robinson Crusoe*, "They are proud, like *men!*" It should be clear from our analysis of his supposedly atheistic humanism that it is not a closed view of man, limiting human potential for the sheer spite of excluding an unwanted God. Bunuel's humanism places no such limits upon man, but rather demonstrates that when God is dead, as Bonhoeffer said, "man comes of age." Whether this is interpreted to mean that man assumes the terrible responsibilities formerly attributed to God, or simply that man now reveals his potential to become God, the effect is much the same. In either case, Bunuel will not call God down into existence merely to save, to prop up, his personal concerns. He has too much respect for God to do that.

The intensely personal nature of his films not only focuses our attention on their author, but at times actually portrays Bunuel in a way that may shed light on his work of demythologizing a post-Christian culture. At times Bunuel is like the blind beggar in *Los Olvidados,* striking about him with his deadly cane at threatening forces. His lack of faith gives him a vulnerability that

compels us to tolerate his terrible blows at our beliefs. At
other times Bunuel is like the pathetic Uncle Jaime of
Viridiana, making films that, like Uncle Jaime's suicide
note, will bind the Church (the niece) to him, even in
death. Those who pity Bunuel liken him to the dirty old
man in *Diary of a Chambermaid,* calling on the servant
girls to try on his collection of boots. But I prefer to see
him at the peak of his career in *Robinson Crusoe,* a
lonely exile shouting to a God who only echoes his own
voice. Today, Bunuel has come to grips with his age, and
he has had the courage to incorporate himself into the
image of Don Lope of *Tristana,* a proud anticlerical now
keeping company with a clutch of clerics talking small
talk. If we were to extend the analogy, we might even
include Catherine Deneuve as the elusive beauty for
which he searched, and by which he was destroyed. Not
only do these characters speak with Bunuel's voice, but
many of them have their creator's own tormented countenance, like the blind beggar of *Viridiana.*

During one temptation in *Simon of the Desert,* the
devil says to Simon, "We're not so different, we two." It
would be difficult for any believer not to experience
some sense of comradeship with the "devil" Bunuel.
After all, he shares so many of our human concerns that
we could hardly reject his sense of outrage, especially
when it kindles our own concern. For this reason, we can
apply to Bunuel Emerson Shideler's apologia for the
Death of God theologians:

> Those today who, from within the environment of Chris-
> tian theology, announce the death of God put themselves
> forth as the saviors of the tradition, not its funeral orators.
> They declare the death of God, not in order to get rid of
> religion, which stands in the way of man's fulfillment, but
> in order to release that religious faith and its institutions to
> do its work. Unlike Caesar's mourners, they have come to
> bury God, not to praise him, in order to do God's work
> which, they say, cannot be accomplished so long as men
> believe that he is still alive.

Before those of us who defend the orthodoxy and guard
the purity of the covenant community consign these
strange voices to the Samaria reserved for those of mixed
blood and confused faith, we should pay some attention to
what they have to say. It behooves those of us who are not
prepared to attend God's funeral to be clearer than we have
been about what we mean when we use the divine name. [3]

Luis Bunuel does not set out to save a tradition, but
his surgeon's hand may make the recovery of religion a
possibility. For this reason, and for many others, we
should listen to what he says. Bunuel once remarked, "I
ask that a film discover something for me." It is reason-
able to expect the same of his works, and one is seldom
disappointed in this regard, even when his films appear as
a prolonged demythologization ending in the Death of
God. He has taken us into the Passion of moral ambiguity, where we can no longer enjoy the luxury of being
certain about the cosmic struggle between good and evil,
and where we can no longer be sure of our role in that
struggle. He has also introduced us to the Death which is
secularization, a world without God, in which man has
outgrown his religious adolescence. Is there also a Resur-
rection discernible in Bunuel's life work? We cannot say
for sure. However, the felt absence of God which perme-
ates his work is at least as effective as the empty tomb to
demonstrate the victory over death. All that is necessary
is the voice of an angel, not an "exterminating angel,"
but one who will announce that Christ goes before us to
prepare a place for us.

In 1955, Bunuel made a film for which he chose the
title *Cela s'Appelle l'Aurore*. The phrase is taken from
Jean Giraudoux's *Electra:*

Is there a name for the moment when the day breaks, as
today, when everything is ruined, ravaged, yet the air is still

---

3. "God is Dead Myth," an unpublished address to the Iowa Theological
Conference, Iowa State College, Cedar Falls, Iowa, January 29, 1966.

fresh, and when everything has failed, and the city burns, and the innocents are driven to slaughter one another, but the guilty lie dying, in a corner of the new day? It has a beautiful name. It is called, Dawn. . . .[4]

Bunuel's works add up to a new beginning, a dawn of the cold, white light in which we can see clearly what has been done on earth in God's name, and in which we can perhaps do something about it. The scandal of evil leads to rebellion, even to the rebellion of declaring God dead. The gospel according to Bunuel is not a mindless parody, but a sensitive critique which all believers can study and reflect upon. If it is true, as Altizer has said, that "only a Christian can experience the death of God," then Bunuel's account of the passing of the deity is a daring act of faith. His supreme service has been to demand better myths for our time, to replace the old myths that dehumanize us. And even if he leaves no plan for doing this, he has opened up the constraining myths of man to allow the human potential of freedom to emerge without the restraint even of an atheistic humanism.

Harvey Cox summarizes the Death of God movement and its effect on the future of theology in a few sentences:

> The "death of God" syndrome signals the collapse of the static orders and fixed categories by which men have understood themselves in the past. It opens the future in a new and radical way. . . . One could never weep for a dead god. A god who can die deserves no tears. Rather, we would rejoice that, freed of another incubus, we now take up the task of fashioning a future made possible not by anything that "is," but by "He who comes."[5]

To this, we can hopefully presume, Bunuel would reply with his unique motto, "I am still an atheist, thank God!"

4. Quoted without reference by Durgnat, *Luis Bunuel*, p. 100.
5. "The Death of God and the Future of Theology," p. 253.

Filmography

In France

1926 Assistant director Mauprat (Jean Epstein).

1927 Assistant director: *La Sirène des Tropiques* (Mario Nalpas and Etiévant).

1928 Assistant director: *La Chute de la Maison Usher* (Jean Epstein).

UN CHIEN ANDALOU
Produced: Luis Bunuel, Pierre Braunberger. *Script:* Bunuel and Salvador Dali. *Photographed:* Albert Dubergen (Duverger). *Edited:* Bunuel. *Sets:* Schilzneck. *Music* (soundtrack added in 1960): from Wagner's *Tristan und Isolde,* and an Argentinian tango. *Cast:* Simone Mareuil, Pierre Batcheff, Jaime Miravilles, Salvador Dali, Luis Bunuel.

1930 L'AGE D'OR
Produced: Vicomte de Noailles, Pierre Braunberger. *Script:* Bunuel (and, nominally, Salvador Dali). *Photographed:* Albert Dubergen. *Edited:* Bunuel. *Sets:* Schilzneck. *Music:* Georges Van Parys, with extracts from Wagner, Beethoven, Mendelssohn and Debussy. *Cast:* Gaston Modot, Lya Lys, Max Ernst, Pierre Prévert, Jose Artigas, Caridad de Lamberdesque.

In Spain

1932 LAS HURDES (TIERRA SINPAN) (English title *Land Without Bread)*
Produced: Ramon Acin. *Script:* Bunuel. *Assistant directors:* Pierre Unik, Sanchez Ventura. *Commentary:* Pierre Unik. *Photographed:* Eli Lotar. *Edited:* Bunuel. *Music:* extracts from Brahms and Mendelssohn.

1935 Executive producer: *Don Quentin el Amargao* (Luis Marquina). Executive producer: *La Hija de Juan Simon* (Jose Luis Saenz de Heredia).
1936 Executive producer: *Quien me quiere a mi?* (Jose Luis Saenz de Heredia). Executive producer: *Centinela! Alerta!* (Jean Grémillon, completed by Bunuel).
1937 Collaborated on documentary *Espana Leal en Armas* (the section *Madrid 36*). Supervised *Espagne 39* (Jean-Paul le Chanois).

In the U.S.A.

1939-42 Propaganda films.
1946 Worked on script of *The Beast with Five Fingers,* directed by Robert Florey.

In Mexico

1947 GRAN CASINO (EN EL VIEJO TAMPICO)
Produced: Oscar Dancigers. *Story:* Michael Weber. *Adaptation:* Mauricio Magdaleno. *Dialogue:* Javier Mateos. *Photographed:* Jack Draper. *Sets:* Javier Torres Torija. *Edited:* Gloria Schoeman. *Music:* Manuel Esperon. *Cast:* Libertad Lamarque, Jorge Negrete, Mercedes Barba, Augustin Isunza, Julio Villareol, Charles Rooner.

1949 EL GRAN CALAVERA
Produced: Oscar Dancigers. *Script:* Raquel Rojas, Luis Alcoriza, after a comedy by Adolfo Torrado. *Photographed:* Ezequiel Carrasco. *Sets:* Luis Moya and Dario Cabanas. *Edited:* Carlos Savage. *Music:* Manuel Esperon. *Cast:* Fernando Soler, Rosario Granados, Ruben Rojo, Andres Soler, Maruja Crufell, Gustavo Rojo, Luis Alcoriza.

1950 LOS OLVIDADOS (English title *The Young and the Damned*)
Produced: Oscar Dancigers. *Script:* Luis Bunuel and Luis Alcoriza. *Photographed:* Gabriel Figueroa. *Sets:* Edward Fitzgerald. *Edited:* Carlos Savage. *Music:* Rodolfo Halffter, on themes of Gustavo Pittaluga. *Cast:* Estela Inda Miguel Inclan, Roberto Cobo, Alfonso Mejia, Hector Lopez Portillo, Salvador Quiros, Victor Manuel Mendoza, Alma Delia Fuentes.

SUSANA (DEMONIO Y CARNE)
Produced: Oscar Dancigers. *Script:* Jaime Salvador, after a

novel by Manuel Reachi. *Photographed:* Jose Ortiz Ramos.
Sets: Gunter Gerzso. *Edited:* Jorge Bustos. *Music:* Raul La-
vista. *Cast:* Rosita Quintana, Fernando Soler, Victor Manuel
Mendoza, Matilde Palau.

1951 LA HIJA DEL ENGANO (DON QUINTIN EL AMARGAO)
Produced: Oscar Dancigers. *Script:* Raquel Rojas, Luis Al-
coriza, after the play *Don Quintin el Amargao* by Carlos
Arniches. *Photographed:* Jose Ortiz Ramos. *Sets:* Edward
Fitzgerald. *Edited:* Carlos Savage. *Music:* Manuel Esperon.
Cast: Fernando Soler, Alicia Caro, Ruben Rojo, Nacho Con-
tra, Fernando Soto, Lily Aclemar.

UNA MUJER SIN AMOR
Produced: Oscar Dancigers. *Script:* Jaime Salvador, after Guy
de Maupassant's novel *Pierre et Jean. Photographed:* Raul
Martinez Solares. *Sets:* Gunter Gerzso. *Edited:* Jorge Bustos.
Music: Raul Larista. *Cast:* Rosario Granados, Julio Villareal,
Tito Junco, Joaquin Cordero.

SUBIDA AL CIELO (English title *Mexican Bus Ride*)
Produced: Manuel Altolaguirre. *Script:* Manuel Altolaguirre,
Juan la Cabado, Bunuel, after a story by Manuel Altolaguirre.
Dialogue: Juan de la Cabada. *Photographed:* Alex Philips.
Sets: Edward Fitzgerald, Jose Rodriguez Granada. *Edited:*
Rafael Portillo. *Music:* Gustavo Pittaluga. *Cast:* Lilia Prado,
Carmelita Gonzales, Esteban Marquez, Manuel Donde,
Roberto Cobo, Acevez Castenada.

1952 EL BRUTO
Produced: Oscar Dancigers. *Script:* Bunuel, Luis Alcoriza.
Photographed: Augustin Jimenez. *Sets:* Gunter Gerzso.
Edited: Jorge Bustos. *Music:* Raul Lavista. *Cast:* Pedro Ar-
mendariz, Katy Jurado, Rosita Arenas, Andres Soler, Rober-
to Meyer.

THE ADVENTURES OF ROBINSON CRUSOE
Produced: Oscar Dancigers, Henry F. Ehrlich. *Script:* Bunuel,
Philip Roll, after the novel by Daniel Defoe. *Photographed*
(colour): Alex Philips. *Sets:* Edward Fitzgerald. *Edited:* Car-
los Savage, Alberto Valenzuela. *Music:* Anthony Collins.
Cast: Dan O'Herlihy, Jaime Fernandez, Felipe de Alba, Chel
Lopez, Jose Chaves, Emilio Garibay.

EL
Produced: Oscar Dancigers. *Script:* Bunuel, Luis Alcoriza,
after *Pensamientos* by Mercedes Pinto. *Photographed:* Gabriel

Figueroa. *Sets:* Edward Fitzgerald. *Edited:* Carlos Savage. *Music:* Luis Hernandes Breton. *Cast:* Arturo de Cordova, Delia Garces, Luis Beristain, Aurora Walker, Manuel Donde, Martinez Baena.

1953 CUMBRES BORRASCOSAS (ABISMOS DE PASION)
Produced: Oscar Dancigers. *Script:* Bunuel, Arduino Maiuri and Julio Alejandro, after *Wuthering Heights* by Emily Bronte. *Photographed:* Augustin Jimenez. *Sets:* Edward Fitzgerald. *Edited:* Carlos Savage. *Music:* Raul Lavista, excerpts from Wagner. *Cast:* Irasema Dilian, Jorge Mistral, Lilia Prado, Ernesto Alonso, Luis Aceves Castenada, Francisco Requeira.

LA ILUSION VIAJA EN TRANVIA
Produced: Armando Orive Alba. *Script:* Mauricio de la Serna, Jose Revueltas, based on a story by Mauricio de la Serna. *Photographed:* Raul Martinez Solares. *Sets:* Edward Fitzgerald. *Edited:* Jorge Bustos. *Music:* Luis Hernandes Breton. *Cast:* Lilia Prado, Carlos Navarro, Domingo Soler, Fernando Soto, Augustin Isunza, Miguel Manzano, Javier de la Parra, Guillermo Bravo Soso, Felipe Montojo.

1954 EL RIO Y LA MUERTE
Produced: Armando Orive Alba. *Script:* Bunuel, Luis Alcoriza, after the novel *Muro Blanco en Roca Negra* by Miguel Alvarez Acosta. *Photographed:* Raul Martinez Solares. *Sets:* Edward Fitzgerald, Gunter Gerzso. *Edited:* Jorge Bustos. *Music:* Raul Lavista. *Cast:* Columba Dominguez, Miguel Torruco, Joaquin Cordero, Jaime Fernandez, Victor Alcover.

1955 LA VIDA CRIMINAL DE ARCHIBALDO DE LA CRUZ (ENSAYO DE UN CRIMEN)
Produced: Alfonso Patino Gomez. *Script:* Bunuel, Eduardo Ugarte, after the novel *Ensayo de un Crimen* by Rodolfo Usigli. *Photographed:* Augustin Jimenez. *Sets:* Jesus Bracho. *Edited:* Pablo Gomez. *Music:* Jorge Perez Herrera. *Cast:* Ernesto Alonso, Miroslava Stern, Rita Macedo, Adriana Welter, Rodolfo Landra, Andrea Palma, Carlos Riquelme, J. Maria Linares Rivas, Leonor Llansas.

In France

CELA S'APPELLE L'AURORE
Produced: André Cultet. *Script:* Bunuel, Jean Ferry, after

the novel by Emmanuel Roblès. *Dialogue:* Jean Ferry. *Photographed:* Robert le Febvre. *Sets:* Max Douy. *Edited:* Marguerite Renoir. *Music:* Joseph Kosma. *Cast:* Georges Marchal, Lucia Bose, Giani Esposito, Julien Bertheau, Nelly Borgeaud, Jean-Jacques Delbo, Robert Le Fort, Brigitte Elloy, Henri Nassiet, Gaston Modot.

In Mexico

1956 LA MORT EN CE JARDIN (English title *Evil Eden*)
   Produced: Oscar Dancigers. *Script:* Bunuel, Luis Alcoriza, Raymond Queneau, after the novel by José-André Lacour. *Dialogue:* Raymond Queneau, Gabriel Arout. *Photographed* (colour): Jorge Stahl, Jr. *Sets:* Edward Fitzgerald. *Edited:* Marguerite Renoir. *Music:* Paul Misraki. *Cast:* Georges Marchal, Simone Signoret, Michel Piccoli, Michèle Girardon, Charles Vanel, Tito Junco.

1958 NAZARIN
   Produced: Manuel Barbachano Ponce. *Script:* Bunuel, Julio Alejandro, after the novel by Benito Perez Galdos. *Photographed:* Gabriel Figueroa. *Sets:* Edward Fitzgerald. *Edited:* Carlos Savage. *Cast:* Francisco Rabal, Marga Lopez, Rita Macedo, Jesus Fernandez, Ignacio Lopez-Tarso, Ofelia Guilmàin, Noe Muragama, Luis Aceves Castenada.

1959 LA FIEVRE MONTE A EL PAO (English title *Republic of Sin*)
   Produced: Raymond Borderie. *Script:* Luis Alcoriza, Bunuel, Charles Dorat, Louis Sapin, after the novel by Henry Castillou. *Dialogue:* Louis Sapin. *Photographed:* Gabriel Figueroa. *Sets:* Jorge Fernandez. *Edited:* James Guenet. *Music:* Paul Misraki. *Cast:* Gerard Philipe, Maria Felix, Jean Servais, M.A. Ferres, Raoul Dantes, Domingo Soler, Victor Junco, Roberto Canedo.

1960 THE YOUNG ONE (ISLAND OF SHAME)
   Produced: George P. Werker. *Script:* Bunuel, H.B. Addis, after the novel *Travelin' Man* by Peter Matthiessen. *Photographed:* Gabriel Figueroa. *Sets:* Jesus Bracho. *Edited:* Carlos Savage. *Music:* Jesus Zarzosa, Leon Bibb. *Cast:* Kay Meersman, Bernie Hamilton, Zachary Scott, Claudio Brook, Graham Denton.

In Spain

1961 VIRIDIANA
Produced: Gustavo Alatriste. *Script:* Bunuel, Jorge Alejandro. *Photographed:* Jose F. Aguayo. *Sets:* Francisco Canet. *Edited:* Pedro Del Rey. *Music:* Hallelujah Chorus from Handel's *Messiah. Cast:* Francisco Rabal, Sylvia Pinal, Fernando Rey, Margarita Lozano, Victoria Zinny, Teresa Rabal, Jose Calvo, Joaquin Roa, Luis Heredia, Jose Manuel Martin, Dolores Gaos, Juan Garcia Tienda, Maruja Isbert, Joaquin Mayol, Palmira Guerra, Servio Mendizabal, Milagros Tomas, Alicia J. Barriga.

1962 EL ANGEL EXTERMINADOR
Produced: Gustavo Alatriste. *Script:* Bunuel, after a screenplay by Bunuel and Luis Alcoriza, *Les Naufrages de la Rue de la Providence* (based on the play *Los Naufragos* by Jose Benjamin). *Photographed:* Gabriel Figueroa. *Sets:* Jesus Bracho. *Edited:* Carlos Savage. *Music:* excerpts from Dominico Scarlatti and a sonata by Paradisi. *Cast:* Sylvia Pinal, Enrique Rembal, Jaqueline Andere, Jose Baviera, Augusto Benedico, Luis Beristain, Antonio Bravo, Claudio Brook, Cesar Del Campo, Rosa Elena Durgel, Lucy Gallardo, Enrique Garcia Alvarez, Ofelia Guilmain, Nadia Haro Oliva, Tito Junco, Xavier Loya, Xavier Masse, Angel Merino, Ofelia Montesco, Patricia Moran, Patricia de Morelos, Bertha Moss.

In France

1964 LE JOURNAL D'UNE FEMME DE CHAMBRE (English title *Diary of a Chambermaid*)
Produced: Serge Silberman and Michel Safra. *Script:* Bunuel, Jean-Claude Carrière, after the novel by Octave Mirbeau. *Photographed* (Franscope): Roger Fellous. *Sets:* Georges Wakhévitch. *Edited:* Louisette Hautecoeur. *Cast:* Jeanne Moreau, Michel Piccoli, Georges Geret, Francoise Lugagne, Jean Ozenne, Daniel Ivernel, Marguerite Dubourg.

1965 SIMON OF THE DESERT
Produced: Gustavo Alatriste. *Script:* Bunuel. *Photographed:* Gabriel Figueroa. *Music:* Raul Lavista. *Cast:* Claudio Brook, Sylvia Pinal, Hortensia Santovena, Francisco Reiguera.

1966 BELLE DE JOUR
Produced: Robert and Raymond Hakim. *Script:* Luis Bunuel

and Jean-Claude Carrière, based on the novel by Joseph Kessel of the Academie Francaise. *Photographed:* Sacha Vierny. *Sets:* Maurice Barnathan. *Edited:* Louisette Hautecoeur. *Cast:* Catherine Deneuve, Jean Sorel, Michel Piccoli, Genevieve Page, Francisco Rabal, Pierre Clementi, Francoise Fabian, Maria Latour, Francis Blanche, Georges Marchal, Francoise Maistre, Macha Meril, Muni, Dominique Dandrieux.

1970 LA VOIE LACTEE (English title *The Milky Way*)
Produced: Serge Silberman. *Script:* Bunuel and Jean-Claude Carrière. *Photographed:* Christian Matras. *Sets:* Pierre Guffray. *Edited:* Louisette Hautecoeur. *Cast:* Paul Frankeur, Laurent Terzieff, Michel Piccoli, Pierre Clementi, Georges Marchal, Claudio Brook, Delphine Seyrig, Michel Etcheverry, Alain Cuny, Edith Scob, Bernard Verley, Francois Maistre, Claude Cerval, Muni, Julien Bertheau, Jean Piat, Denis Manuel, Daniel Pilon, Marcel Peres.

1971 TRISTANA
Produced: Papagallo-Torres. *Script:* Luis Bunuel and Julio Alejandro, from the novel by Benito Perez Galdos. *Photographed:* Roger Aguayo. *Edited:* Pedro Delres. *Cast:* Catherine Deneuve, Fernando Rey, Franco Nero, Lola Galos, Jesus Fernandez.

1972 THE DISCREET CHARM OF THE BOURGEOISIE
Produced: Serge Silberman. Story and screenplay by Bunuel and Jean-Claude Carrière. *Photographed:* Edmond Richard. *Sets:* Pierre Guffroy. *Edited:* Helene Plemiannikov. *Cast:* Fernando Rey, Jean-Pierre Cassel, Delphine Seyrig, Paul Frankeur, Stephane Audran, Bulle Ogier, Julien Bertheau, Claude Pieplu, Michel Piccoli.

Rental Sources for Bunuel Films

Although Luis Bunuel's major works are available in 16mm from several sources, a number of his lesser films have not found a distributor at the time of this writing. Many of the films are known by several titles, some of them in different languages, and so these have been included to facilitate the task of locating these films. Prices have not been included because they are frequently assigned according to type of screening, size of audience, and admission charges. The vagaries of 16mm film distribution have, unfortunately, made it impossible to locate a source for THE MILKY WAY.

UN CHIEN ANDALOU (France, 1928; 20min; b/w; silent or added sound) Audio/Brandon Films, Museum of Modern Art

L'AGE D'OR (France, 1930; b/w; silent or sound added) distributor unknown.

LAS HURDES (Spain, 1932; 31min; b/w; sound) Contemporary Films/McGraw-Hill, Museum of Modern Art

GRAN CASINO *(En El Viejo Tampico)* (Mexico, 1947; 85min; b/w) distributor unknown

EL GRAN CALAVERA (Mexico, 1949; 90min; b/w) distributor unknown

LOS OLVIDADOS *(The Young & the Damned)* (Mexico, 1950; 88min; b/w) Audio/Brandon Films

SUSANA *(Demonio y Carne)* (Mexico, 1951; 82min; b/w) distributor unknown

LA HIJA DEL ENGANO *(Don Quintin el Amargao)* (Mexico, 1951; 80min; b/w) distributor unknown

UNA MUJER SIN AMOR (Mexico, 1951; b/w) (Spanish only) Azteca Films, Inc.

MEXICAN BUS RIDE *(Subida al Cielo)* (Mexico, 1951; 85min; b/w) Contemporary Films/McGraw-Hill

EL BRUTO (Mexico, 1952; 83min; b/w) distributor unknown

ROBINSON CRUSOE (The Adventures of . . .) (Mexico, 1952; 89min; color) St. Paul Films

THIS STRANGE PASSION *(El)* (Mexico, 1952; 82min; b/w) Audio/Brandon Films

CUMBRAS BORRASCOSAS *(Abismos de Pasion)* (Mexico, 1953; 90min; b/w) distributor unknown

LA ILUSION VIAJA EN TRANVIA (Mexico, 1953; 90min; b/w) distributor unknown

EL RIO Y LA MUERTE (Mexico, 1954; 90min; b/w) (Spanish only) Azteca Films, Inc.

ENSAYO DE UN CRIMEN *(The Criminal Life of Archibaldo de La Cruz)* (Mexico, 1955; 91min; b/w) distributor unknown

CELA S'APPELLE L'AURORE (France-Italy, 1955; 102min; b/w) distributor unknown

LA MORT EN CE JARDIN *(Evil Eden)* (France-Mexico, 1956; 97min; b/w) distributor unknown

NAZARIN (Mexico, 1958; 94min; b/w) Audio/Brandon Films

LA FIEVRE MONTE A EL PAO *(Los Ambiciosos, Republic of Sin)* (France-Mexico, 1959; 97min; b/w) distributor unknown
THE YOUNG ONE *(La Joven, Island of Shame)* (Mexico, 1960; 95min; b/w) distributor unknown
VIRIDIANA (Spain-Mexico, 1961; 90min; b/w) Audio/Brandon Films
EL ANGEL EXTERMINADOR *(The Exterminating Angel)* (Mexico, 1962; 95min; b/w) Audio/Brandon Films
LE JOURNAL D'UNE FEMME DE CHAMBRE *(Diary of a Chambermaid)* (France-Italy, 1964; 95min; b/w) Films Incorporated
SIMON DEL DESIERTO *(Simon of the Desert)* (Mexico, 1965; 42min; b/w) Audio/Brandon Films
BELLE DE JOUR (France, 1966; color) Hurlock Cine World
THE MILKY WAY *(La Voie Lactee)* (France-Spain, 1970; color) distributor unknown; U-M Productions (35mm)
TRISTANA (Spain, 1971; color) Audio/Brandon Films
THE DISCREET CHARM OF THE BOURGEOISIE (France, 1972; 100min; color) U.S. release by Twentieth Century Fox; 16mm distributor unknown

Audio/Brandon Films
        Main Office: 34 Mac Questen Parkway, South Mount Vernon, N.Y. 10550 (914) 664-5051
        Exchanges: Baltimore, Boston, Buffalo, Chicago, Dallas, Denver, Honolulu, Indianapolis, Kansas City, Los Angeles, Memphis, Miami, Milwaukee, Minneapolis, New York City, Portland, Richmond, San Francisco, St. Louis.

Azteca Films, Inc.
        Main Office: 132 West 43rd Street, New York, N.Y. 10036 (212) 695-4740

Contemporary Films/McGraw-Hill
        Main Office: 1221 Ave. of the Americas, New York, N.Y. 10020 (212) 997-6436
        Exchanges: 828 Custer Avenue, Evanston, Illinois 60202 (312) 869-5010; 1714 Stockton Street, San Francisco, Calif. 94133 (415) 362-3115

Films Incorporated
>   Main Office: 4420 Oakton Street, Skokie, Illinois
>   60076 (312) 676-1088
>   Exchanges: Atlanta, Boston, Chicago, Dallas, Holly-
>   wood, New York, Portland, Salt Lake
>   City, San Diego.

Hurlock Cine World
>   Main Offices: 13 Arcadia Road, Old Greenwich, Conn.
>   06870 (203) 637-4319
>   No Exchanges

Museum of Modern Art
>   Main Office: 11 West 53rd Street, New York, N.Y.
>   10019 (212) 956-2404

St. Paul Films
>   Main Office: Dearborn, Michigan
>   No Exchanges

Bibliography

No comprehensive bibliography of material on or by Luis Bunuel exists at this time. The absence of a complete collection of scripts is probably the most regrettable. The following titles have been selected for their importance and availability from the works of John Russell Taylor, Raymond Durgnat, and especially from Ado Kyrou, whose *Luis Bunuel* contains the most complete bibliography for works written in Europe.

I. SCRIPTS

L'Age d'Or, Un Chien Andalou. Classic Film Scripts, Simon & Schuster, New York, 1968.

Viridiana, Exterminating Angel, Simon of the Desert. Orion Press, New York, 1965.

Belle de Jour. Modern Film Scripts, Simon & Schuster, New York, 1971.

II. BOOKS

Agel, Henry. *Miroirs de l'Insolite dans le Cinema Francais.* Editions du Cerf, Paris, 1958.

Agel, Henry and Ayfre, Amedee. *Le Cinema et le Sacre.* Collection Septieme Art, Editions du Cerf, Paris, 1961; "Dix Ans Plus Tard," pp. 133-137.

Ayfre, Amedee. *Conversion aux Images?* "Bunuel et la Christianisme." Editions du Cerf, Paris, pp. 75-94.

Bazin, Andre. *Qu'est ce que le Cinema?* Vol. 3, *Cinema et Sociologie.* Editions du Cerf, Paris, 1958.

Brunius, Jacques. *Experiment in the Film,* ed. Roger Manvell. Grey Walls Press, London, 1959.

Buache, Freddy. *Luis Bunuel.* Premier Plan No. 13. 1960.

Luis Bunuel. Premier Plan No. 33. 1964.

Cox, Harvey. "The Death of God and the Future of Theology," *New Theology* No. 4, ed., Martin Marty & Dean G. Peerman. Macmillan and Company, New York, 1967.

Dali, Salvador. *The Secret Life of Salvador Dali.* Dial Press, New York, 1942. Vision Press, 1948.

Durgnat, Raymond. *Luis Bunuel.* University of California Press, Berkeley, 1968.

Hunt, Albert, in *Film Teaching,* by Harcourt & Whannel, B.F.I., 1965.

Hurley, Neil. *Theology Through Film.* Harper & Row, New York, 1970.

Kael, Pauline. *Going Steady.* Little, Brown & Company, Boston, 1968. "Saintliness *(Simon of the Desert),"* pp. 254-262.

Kyrou, Ado. *Luis Bunuel.* Editions Seghers: Cinema D'Aujourd'hui, Paris, 1962. Simon & Schuster, 1963.

Le Surrealisme au Cinema, 2nd ed. Le Terrain Vague, Paris, 1963.

Lizalde, Eduardo. *Luis Bunuel.* Cuadernos de Cine, No. 2, 1962.

Lovell, Alan. *Anarchist Cinema.* Peace News, B.F.I., 1963.

Miller, Henry. *The Cosmological Eye.* Editions Poetry, Nicholson & Watson, London, 1945.

Rebolledo, Carlos and Frederic Grange. *Bunuel.* Editions Universitaires, Paris, 1965.

Sarris, Andrew. *Confessions of a Cultist: On the Cinema, 1955-1969.* Simon & Schuster, New York, 1971. "Viridiana," pp. 53-60. "Belle de Jour," pp. 353-359.

Taylor, John Russell. *Cinema Eye, Cinema Ear: Some Key Film*

Makers of the Sixties. Hill & Wang, New York, 1964. "Bunuel," pp. 82-114.
Tyler, Parker. *Underground Film: A Critical History.* Grove Press, New York, 1969.

III. SPECIAL ISSUES OF MAGAZINES
Film Culture, No. 41 (Summer 1946).
Cahiers du Cinema, No. 7 (December 1951).
Positif, No. 10 (1954).
Image et Son, No. 119 (December, 1958).
Positif, No. 42 (1961).
Nuevo Cine, Nos. 4-5 (November, 1961).
Image et Son, No. 157 (December, 1962).
Etudes Cinematographiques, Nos. 20-21, 22-23 (1963).
L'Avant-Scene du Cinema, No. 36 (April, 1964).

IV. MAGAZINE ARTICLES
Aranda, J.F. "Back from the Wilderness," *Films and Filming* (November, 1961). "Bunuel Espagnol," *Cinema 57* (December, 1957). "Surrealist and Spanish Giant," *Films and Filming* (October, 1961).
Borde, Ciment and Demeure. "Les Inedits de Luis Bunuel," *Positif*, No. 75 (May, 1966).
Bunuel, Juan. "A Letter by Juan Bunuel on *The Exterminating Angel*," *Film Culture*, No. 41 (Summer, 1946).
Harcourt, Peter. "Luis Bunuel: Spaniard & Surrealist," *Film Quarterly* (Spring, 1967).
Kanesaka, Kenji. "A Visit to Bunuel," *Film Culture*, No. 41 (Summer, 1946).
Kyrou, Ado, Martin, Seguin, and Thirard. "Sur Nazarin," *Positif*, No. 33.
Seguin, Louis. "Viridiana et Les Critiques," *Positif*, No. 47 (July, 1962).